THE
COMPLETE BOOK OF
CONSULTING

THE
COMPLETE BOOK OF
CONSULTING

Written by
Bill Salmon and Nate Rosenblatt

Round Lake Publishing

Round Lake Publishing Co.
31 Bailey Avenue
Ridgefield, CT 06877

Printed in the United States of America

0   9   8   7   6   5   4

ISBN 0-929543-44-0

DEDICATION

Special thanks to my wife/partner, Rosemary, for hours of technical help and advice with this book, for her courage and strength during her recent illness, and for a lifetime of encouragement and support. —Bill Salmon

Thanks and appreciation to my wife (and editor) who has an unerring eye for accuracy and truth. —Nate Rosenblatt

Acknowledgments

Many thanks to Bert David (The Lead Alliance), and Lynne Weaver (J&L Computer Service), two colleagues who shared many of their success secrets, forms and proposals. Thanks also to Rich Grossman (Motorola), Dave Gross (Gorca Systems, Inc.) and many other friends and associates who offered their valuable time and insights.

Other Helpful Books from Round Lake Publishing

The following books are available from your bookseller. If they are not in stock, you may order directly from Round Lake Publishing.

Complete Book of Contemporary Business Letters
400 model letters for all areas of business, including customer relations, handling customer complaints, credit and collections, personnel relations, memos and reports, job search, personal letters and much more. 470 pages, soft cover, 6" x 8 3/4" $19.95

The Only Personal Letter Book You'll Ever Need
Over 400 letters cover all areas of personal correspondence, including apologies and thank you's, complaints to companies and individuals, congratulations and invitations, saying no, sympathy and condolences, and much more. *"Covers almost any occasion known to man...the perfect solution for those sticky moments."*—Newsweek. 460 pages, soft cover, 6" x 8 3/4" $19.95

Hiring, Firing (and everything in between) Personnel Forms Book
160 forms covering all aspects of personnel management, including job applications, interviewing guides, personnel policies, performance appraisals, orientation, attendance, salary, discipline, benefits, termination, federal regulations, and more. 370 pages, soft cover, 6" x 8 3/4" $19.95

Step-By-Step Legal Forms and Agreements
165 legal forms for business and personal use. Includes wills, living will, power of attorney, forms for buying and selling real estate, starting a company, corporate forms, and much more. The most comprehensive book of its kind. *"Could hardly be easier to use"*—The New York Times. 440 pages, soft cover, 6" x 8 3/4" $19.95

Encyclopedia of Money Making Sales Letters
Over 300 letters covering all phases of selling, from prospecting for new customers to closing sales. Includes responses to objections, keeping the customer buying, selling yourself, plus much more. *"Helps sell anything"*—The New York Times. 370 pages, soft cover, 6" x 8 3/4" $19.95

Order Form

consl

Please rush me the following books:
- ☐ Complete Book of Contemporary Business Letters $19.95
- ☐ The Only Personal Letter Book You'll Ever Need $19.95
- ☐ Hiring, Firing (and everything in between) Personnel Forms Book.................... $19.95
- ☐ Step-By-Step Legal Forms and Agreements $19.95
- ☐ Encyclopedia of Money Making Sales Letters $19.95

Add $3.95 to the total order for shipping

I have enclosed ☐ Check　　Bill my credit card　☐ Am Ex　☐ Visa　☐ MasterCard

Credit card # _____ Exp. Date _____

Signature (required for credit card) _____

Name _____
　　　　Please print
Company _____

Address _____

City _____ State _____ Zip _____

Round Lake Publishing
31 Bailey Avenue, Ridgefield, CT 06877　　　　　　　**(203) 438-6303**

Contents

CHAPTER 3   SETTING YOUR FEES

CHAPTER 4   MARKETING—DIRECT METHODS

Forms

CHAPTER 5   MARKETING—INDIRECT METHODS

Forms

CHAPTER 6   INTERVIEWING PROSPECTS

Forms

CHAPTER 7 DEVELOPING PROPOSALS

Forms

CHAPTER 8 PREPARING CONTRACTS

CHAPTER 9 CREDIT AND COLLECTIONS

CHAPTER 10 RECORD KEEPING FORMS

What this Book Will Do for You

Being an expert in your field does not automatically ensure that you are prepared to run a successful consulting practice. The "business of consulting" is just that—a business. And imparting your knowledge and expertise is just a small part of running that business.

This book will show you exactly how to accomplish all the steps in the consulting process so that you succeed in your business. It will do that by providing a how-to text plus 150 documents, prepared by experts, which help you avoid the trial-and-error approach that eats up so much valuable time.

You'll find out how to start a consulting practice—from picking a location and a name, to deciding on whether to incorporate, to creating a business plan.

Then there's the critical matter of marketing your services. You'll discover how to find qualified prospects and convince them of your abilities. You'll learn how to determine your fee structure, following guidelines that will help you avoid under-charging for your services—or overcharging for them.

Next, you will learn the techniques for interviewing prospects to determine the nature of the project they have in mind, and to decide whether you wish to pursue it. You'll discover how to write winning proposals, a critical step in landing new assignments. You'll see how contracts should be prepared once you get the assignment. And, of course, you'll be given examples of invoices to send, to ensure you get paid for your hard work.

And this is just some of the material you'll find in this unique book.

Every step of the way, you'll not only read explanations of what to do, but you'll be given concrete examples of the forms, letters and other documents you'll need to run a successful consulting business. Even if you are already an established consult-ant, you will find the information and forms invaluable in fine tuning and growing your business.

How to Use this Book

This book covers all aspects of starting and running a successful consulting practice. Each chapter focuses on a specific area of consulting, beginning with hands-on, how-to advice. Whether you're well established or new to the field of consulting, you'll surely profit by reading the text at the beginning of each chapter.

Next, forms, checklists, letters and other documents are shown, giving you expertly crafted, specific examples to use as is—or to customize where necessary. Hints for using and customizing each document are located at the bottom of the page, so that you will get the maximum benefit from each form.

Whatever document you need can be found quickly by using the comprehensive table of contents or either of two indexes, one of which is organized alphabetically and the other which is organized by key word.

Preface

A plumber was called to fix a leak. He looked at the pipe, gripped his hammer with both hands, struck the pipe as hard as he could, and the leak stopped.

He presented the customer with a bill for $250.35. The homeowner was furious. "This is outrageous," he sputtered. "You were here only two minutes and all you did was hit the pipe."

The plumber itemized his bill. Wear and tear on the hammer: 35 cents. Knowing where to hit: $250.00.

This apocryphal story may be as good an example of what consultants do as any: Consultants are paid for knowing what to do—for giving advice.

Stated more formally, consulting is an advisory activity provided by an individual (the consultant) to another individual or group (the client) to meet a specified need within a specified time frame for a specified fee.

Companies hire consultants for a variety of reasons. Primarily, they are:

- To provide an objective, independent viewpoint
- To complete short term projects without adding to staff
- To provide specialized expertise for a specific need
- To provide imaginative solutions for company problems
- To prevent political problems within the client company
- To train client personnel
- To provide sources of capital
- To deal with federal, state or local government
- To act as a catalyst between internal groups

Consulting is one of the fastest growing professions in the country. Revenues for this industry have grown from $1 billion in 1970 to $2 billion in 1980 to well over $3 billion annually in the past several years. The current annual growth rate is approximately 20% and there is no end in sight. For some, these statistics may represent an argument for not entering what seems to be an already overcrowded profession. As many new consultants have discovered, however, there is always room for another talented practitioner. In fact, one of the nicest aspects of the business is that those who are already in it and doing well welcome and help newcomers. Collaboration and cooperation are hallmarks of this profession.

There are many types and sizes of consulting firms, ranging from sole practitioners to the giant accounting firms (all of which have branched out into general consulting) and national management firms. Some consulting businesses specialize in government, and tend to be concentrated in cities, state capitals, and Washington, D.C. Others specialize in specific industries, such as aerospace or utilities. Still others concentrate on one aspect of business (e.g., marketing or management) and cut across all industries.

The variety of services available from consultants has mushroomed during the past several years. A large number of entrepreneurs with highly specialized skills have entered the profession and have found both financial success and job satisfaction. In every type of business there are special competencies and unique services required that consultants, rather than employees, are being asked to provide. And new types of consulting firms appear virtually every day.

As you thumb through this book, you will see solutions to virtually every challenge a new consultant faces—and many that even seasoned consultants must deal with. This book will give you the knowledge, and with it the confidence, to excel in your profession.

Good luck in your consulting practice!

What It Takes to Be a Consultant 1

The first challenge in becoming a successful consultant is to answer two important questions:

- What expertise do I have that others would be willing to pay for?
- Do I have (or could I develop) the required interpersonal skills?

To be successful as a consultant you will need to identify the technical expertise you will offer your clients (**content skills**) and the interpersonal skills you will bring to your consulting relationships (**process skills**).

Content skills include specific knowledge or expertise. For example, you may know the retailing industry, or you may be a mail order specialist, or you may have expertise in the publishing industry.

Content skills also include work skills. To help catalog some of these content skills, think about abilities you have demonstrated in the past. Go back over your academic training and employment experience and list every skill you recognize in yourself or that someone else has recognized in you. Try to be as specific as possible. For example, don't just say "I write well." Say "I write very effective reports." Or don't say "I am very organized" but say instead "I can handle a number of projects simultaneously, and I manage my time so that things get done well before the established deadlines." A Contents Skill Self-Assessment form (1-01) is found at the end of this chapter.

You should be able to come up with a list of both knowledge/expertise content skills and work content skills that can be used as the basis for a consulting practice. Force yourself to combine some of the items on your list into a twenty-five word statement of what you want to do as a consultant. Describe your skills and expertise in a way that will make the most sense to your prospective clients. This is a good chance to practice stating your profession in terms of what you do, not in some non-descriptive, general term ("I am a management consultant").

Here is an example from our own experience. For years, a colleague worked with salespeople in a large international organization. She helped them write proposals, prepare sales presentations, and practice techniques for telephone and face-to-face conversations with prospective customers.

When she decided to start her own business, she at first called herself a "Sales Consultant" and told family, friends, and business associates of her new business. Each time she mentioned her new profession, she was asked to describe what services she performed. Within weeks, the only time she ever used the title was on her business card. From then on, whenever anyone asked what she did for a living, she answered: "I help salespeople sell more of their products and services, so that they and their companies make more money."

What you need to do at this point is to define your content skills in concrete terms: What can you do that will have some measurable benefit for the people who might hire you?

Another way to identify the specific content skills you are planning to offer is based on the famous marketing principle: "Find a need and fill it." Start with a client need and describe how you would meet it. Fill out the Defining Your Services form (1-02) to accomplish this. It's located at the end of the chapter.

Before considering some of the process skills associated with consulting, it would be helpful to take a few minutes to write a brief statement describing the nature of the consulting activity you are considering providing. Work on your statement until you are satisfied it captures (briefly) the essential elements of your area of expertise. There is a Statement of Consulting Services (1-03) at the end of this chapter which you can use.

In addition to content skills, there are a number of process skills that many successful consultants have cited as critical to their success. These skills are divided into five major categories:

1. **Strong communication skills**
   The ability to speak and present well, to write clearly and effectively, and to listen actively are attributes of most outstanding consultants. In fact, many consultants consider the ability to communicate well as the *number one* skill. People with technical degrees are often not schooled in communication skills. If you need help, there are many inexpensive self-help programs available.

2. **Proven problem-solving skills**
   Top consultants understand that the first thing they have to do is define the problem (it's not always what the client thinks it is), and then help the client find a solution. Many potential clients

look for consultants with MBA's because they feel problem-solving skills (known in the business schools as decision analysis) are their stock in trade. However, it's more important to be able to show how your problem-solving ability has positively impacted real-life situations than to wave an advanced degree.

3. **The ability to market yourself**

   It doesn't matter how good you are in your field, and it doesn't matter how specialized or unique your field is. If you can't market yourself, if you can't ask for a sale, you're going to be looking for a new line of work. We've devoted a significant percentage of the documents to this topic because you must be able to tell your story effectively—and sell yourself—if you plan to prosper as a consultant.

4. **Excellent interpersonal skills**

   This is the least tangible of the success skills, but one of the most important. Without a high level of such skills, your chances to win clients—and hold them—are greatly limited. They include your behavior and attitude—in general, how you are perceived by the outside world and, in particular, by your clients. To succeed, you must establish credibility and create a sense of trust and confidence so your clients feel good about selecting you for projects.

5. **The know-how to run your own business efficiently**

   Starting a business requires a certain type of know-how; *managing* and *"growing"* a business require yet another type. As good as they may be in their technical expertise, many consultants don't know how to run a business. The ability to make your consulting business last (and to generate substantial income) requires management skills, which can be learned. If this area is not your strong suit, consider attending extension classes at your local college. Or attend a seminar or two—there are hundreds given around the country each year.

To help you analyze the importance of these process skills, there is a Process Skills Self-Assessment form (1-04) at the end of this chapter. You may find that there are areas for self-improvement that you'll want to work on as you begin your consulting practice.

CONTENT SKILLS SELF-ASSESSMENT

1. I know more about the following subjects than most people:
   a) _____
   b) _____
   c) _____

2. I can do the following things better than most people:
   a) _____
   b) _____
   c) _____

3. I have received the greatest job satisfaction when I have been doing the following things:
   a) _____
   b) _____
   c) _____

4. Family members, employers, coworkers, friends and teachers have told me that I am really good at:
   a) _____
   b) _____
   c) _____

5. I believe people would be willing to pay me for the following:

   Information:

   _____
   _____
   _____

   Skills:

   _____
   _____
   _____

• This form will help you begin thinking about your content skills in concrete terms.

• Focus on what you can provide that will have a measurable benefit for the clients that hire you.

DEFINING YOUR SERVICES

IDENTIFY A NEED	DECIDE IF YOU CAN FILL THE NEED	FILL THE NEED
Why Companies Hire Consultants	Personal Application Questions	Specific Services to Be Offered
1. To save clients time, money, and resources	What do I know how to do better, faster, more cost-effectively than most people? _____ _____ _____	_____ _____ _____ _____ _____ _____ _____
2. To provide an objective, independent viewpoint	Can I give honest, factual, supportive feedback to clients in a potentially hectic, resistant, even hostile environment? _____ _____ _____	_____ _____ _____ _____ _____ _____ _____
3. To complete short term projects which need to be done without adding to staff	Can I provide start-to-finish, high energy commitment to a client project? _____ _____ _____	_____ _____ _____ _____ _____

4. To provide specialized expertise for a present need

What techniques, skills, information do I have that a company may be willing to pay for?

_____
_____
_____
_____
_____
_____
_____
_____

5. To provide imaginative solutions for company problems

How creative can I be as problem-solver, decision maker, catalyst?

_____
_____
_____
_____
_____
_____

6. To provide development opportunities for existing staff members

Can I collaborate successfully with internal staff members in a non-threatening way?

_____
_____
_____
_____
_____
_____
_____

7. To act as a catalyst between internal groups

Can I act as a go-between in a potentially tough environment? How are my team-building and conflict management skills?

_____
_____
_____
_____
_____
_____
_____

- As with the other forms in this chapter, be totally honest with yourself when filling out this document. What you enter will set the stage for your consulting business.

- Don't expect to fill in services for all the numbered items.

STATEMENT OF CONSULTING SERVICES

In the space below, write a short statement (no more than 50 words) describing the kind of consulting service you feel qualified to offer. Review your answers on Forms 1-01 and 1-02 before you begin. The statement should answer the question: "What services will I offer?" in such a way that the benefits to a client can readily be understood by virtually anyone, even if they are not knowledge-able about the field.

Here is the main service I will offer:

_____
_____
_____
_____
_____
_____
_____
_____

• Ask someone whose opinion you trust to read your statement. Listen to their suggestions and revise and refine the statement until you are satisfied with it.

PROCESS SKILLS SELF-ASSESSMENT

5= High
3= Average
1= Low

	My scoring	Friend's scoring of me
Communication Skills		
1. The ability to listen effectively	_____	_____
2. The ability to ask probing questions	_____	_____
3. The ability to ask clarifying questions	_____	_____
4. Effective writing skills	_____	_____
5. Effective verbal communication skills	_____	_____
Analytical Skills		
1. Knowing what's unique about a particular situation	_____	_____
2. Knowing what a situation has in common with others	_____	_____
3. The ability to see the "big picture" and recognize patterns or trends in a series of isolated events	_____	_____
Decision Making Skills		
1. The ability to generate a number of alternatives and evaluate the best ones	_____	_____
2. Cost/benefit analysis skills	_____	_____
Problem Solving Skills		
1. The ability to recognize and deal with causes (not symptoms) of problems	_____	_____
2. The ability to generate creative but workable solutions	_____	_____

Negotiation Skills

1. The ability to define an acceptable position for myself when there is disagreement or conflict   _____   _____

2. The ability to make compromises and reach a comfortable middle ground   _____   _____

Interpersonal Skills/Qualities

1. Empathy; understanding of others   _____   _____
2. Positive thinking   _____   _____
3. High level of energy and enthusiasm   _____   _____

- If you have scored yourself "1" for any question, consider ways you might improve in that area.

- It's helpful to have a friend score you as well, to help determine how others perceive you.

Setting Up
Your Business 2

Determining the Structure of Your Business

The first thing you'll want to do before starting your business is to determine the structure it will take. There are four common structures for a business. The major differences involve the liability of the owners and how the business is taxed.

A **Sole Proprietorship** is a business which is owned and operated by one person. Tax rates for a sole proprietorship are the same as those for an individual. And the sole proprietorship offers no protection to the owner. He or she is liable for any debts of the company.

A **Partnership** is a business structure in which two or more parties jointly own a business. As with a sole proprietorship, partners are taxed as individuals. In addition, the partners accept equal legal responsibility for the company's commitments and debts. A contract should be drawn up between the partners specifying what part of the business each partner owns, the investment each is to make, and what happens if the partnership is terminated, one of the partners dies, or there is a deadlock between the partners. Also, it's a good idea to have a buy-sell agreement, indicating under what terms one party can buy out the interests of the other.

A **C Corporation** is a business entity with a life of its own. A C Corporation limits personal liability since the corporation's owners (the stockholders) usually can lose only their initial investment and any personal assets they use to guarantee or secure loans. A C Corporation makes it possible to transfer ownership of the company through the sale of stock, assets or through a merger. And it provides for the longevity of the company and preserves its continuation beyond the death of any one shareholder. In addition, it is usually easier for a corporation to borrow money or raise capital than it is for other types of businesses.

Corporations are run by boards of directors who are typically elected by the shareholders.

There is a special kind of corporation called an **S Corporation**. Named for Subchapter S of the Internal Revenue Code, this type of corporation is limited to 35 shareholders and generally has the form of a C corporation in all ways except one: The owners are taxed at their individual tax rates instead of at the corporate tax rate. As with a C corporation, the owners are protected, up to the amount of their investment, from other kinds of liability.

There are other financial and operational advantages and disadvantages to each of these forms of business. You certainly will want to discuss all of these options with your financial advisor and attorney before making this important decision. A chart describing the Forms of Business (2-01) is located at the end of the chapter.

You also will probably want to check on other legal matters with your attorney. There may be particular laws or regulations affecting small businesses in your area that you will want to know about and factor into your planning. Depending on the services you choose to provide, you may also need to consider other legal matters such as licenses, patents and copyrights. This information is an important part of your start-up planning.

Choosing Your Location

One of the early decisions you'll need to make is where to locate your practice. To minimize your initial start-up costs and control overhead expenses, you may decide that your home is your best location. This will allow you to save the cost of renting office space. Also, if you designate an area of your home to be used solely for the business, you may be able to deduct part of your rent or mortgage payment from your federal and state income taxes. Discuss this with your financial advisor. If you don't have one, be sure to get a good one right away. An experienced financial advisor and a capable attorney are prerequisites for anyone thinking of starting a business venture.

Giving Your Business a Name

Naming your business is another important consideration. The name of your business will affect the way your customers perceive both you and your business. Your company's name is your initial calling card. It will attract customers looking for the types of services you provide. Ideally, the name should say something about you and the nature of your business. At the very least, it should not confuse prospective clients or make your consulting practice sound insignificant or amateurish.

If you use any business name besides the one you've chosen, you must file a certificate, usually with officials in the town in which you run your business. This is frequently known as a DBA (the abbreviation for "Doing Business As"), or Certificate of Trade Name. A Certificate of Trade Name (2-02) is found later in the chapter.

Creating Your Mission Statement

An important part of setting up your consulting practice is defining your company's business—in relation to its market, the way it operates, how it will compete and its ethical values. The document that communicates the vision—not just to one's self, but to employees and clients—is called the mission statement. Your mission statement helps you focus on what's truly important in your new business, including:

- What business am I in?
- How should it be conducted?
- What gives me a competitive advantage?
- What values guide my actions?

Having a mission statement means that you have a context from which to build marketing strategies and plans. Like any living thing, it will require change as your business grows, but at all times it provides a blueprint from which to work. It defines your business.

A Mission Statement (2-03), and Mission Statement Worksheet (2-04), are found later in this chapter.

Positioning Your Consulting Practice

It doesn't matter if you're a sole practitioner, if you're working out of your home, if you share office space with other individuals, or if you're part of a larger group. You should use the same process giant corporations use to determine their fit in the market. You must be able to define what makes you different from other companies serving the same market and providing the same general services.

Let's suppose you're a computer consultant. Perhaps you're unique because you not only advise clients what software should be purchased, but you also install it and provide the employee training, as well—you're a one-stop source. Perhaps you're unique because you specialize in installation of computer networks, or your company provides 24-hour-a-day trouble shooting. In other words, focus on what specific services you can offer that distinguish you from the others.

In addition to the kinds of services your firm provides, you can position yourself based on:

- Education (e.g., MBA, Ph.D.)

- Price (Why pay for a giant firm's overhead when you can obtain the same service for less?)
- Size (Clients work only with principals)
- Accomplishment (Problem-solving, profit-building experience)

Creating Your Business Plan

Many people—particularly entrepreneurs—think of a business plan as the province of big business. They believe it's only a necessity for large manufacturers, or companies that have substantial cash requirements and must make presentations to bankers and venture capitalists.

But business plans are also crucial to small businesses. And in many ways they're every bit as important as those that large businesses spend hundreds of thousands of dollars to prepare. Business plans help you:

- understand your product or service
- analyze where you're going
- deal with potential problems and pitfalls
- clarify where your financial resources will come from
- measure your growth

A comprehensive business plan can be an invaluable road map: It will give you a sense of purpose and direction; it will help you identify potential roadblocks or detours; and it will give you checkpoints along the way where you can stop to assess the effectiveness of your products, services, and methodologies.

Since a good business plan involves a fairly complete description of your consulting business, including the cost and pricing of your services or products, it will also help you clarify how you want to present yourself to prospective customers. A Business Plan Outline (2-05) and a sample Business Plan (2-06) are shown at the end of the chapter.

FORMS OF BUSINESS

SOLE PROPRIETORSHIP
Definition: A business owned and operated by one individual.

Advantages
- Easy to start
- Least expensive to start
- Owner has greatest control
- Few government restrictions or requirements
- Lowest tax rate of any type of business structure—individual rate

Disadvantages
- Unlimited personal liability
- Growth limited by owner's energy and capabilities
- Business and personal finances can get intermixed
- Often difficult to raise capital or establish credit

PARTNERSHIP
Definition: A business owned and operated by two or more entities.

Advantages
- Income and expenses flow through to partners—taxed as individuals using Schedule K-1
- Opportunity to share financial burdens
- Complementary skills and experience can enhance business

Disadvantages
- Each partner responsible for the total liabilities of partnership
- Can be negatively affected by personal problems of one partner
- Possible disagreements and power struggles between partners
- Often difficult to raise capital or establish credit

CORPORATION

Definition: An entity created by law and owned by stockholders.

C Corporation

Advantages

- Stockholders have no personal liability
- Ownership can be transferred through the sale of stock
- Corporation can survive the death of owners
- Easier to borrow money, raise capital, or establish credit

Disadvantages

- Can be expensive to start
- Heavier tax burden than in other forms of business
- Numerous legal formalities and restrictions
- Required to hold annual meetings and to file financial reports on a regular basis

Subchapter S Corporation

Advantages

- Same tax advantages as Partnerships
- Same limits of liability as C Corporation
- Can borrow money, raise capital as with C Corporation

Disadvantages

- Requires fewer than 35 stockholders and allows no foreign ownership
- Similar disadvantages to setting up and maintaining C Corporation

- When deciding on the form of business to pursue, be sure to seek the advice of both your financial advisor and attorney.

CERTIFICATE OF TRADE NAME

WITNESSETH:

_____, a company having an office at
_____, is as of this date
conducting its business at said address under the name
_____.

In Witness Whereof we have hereunto set our hands and seals this
_____ day of _____, 19__.

Signed, Sealed and Delivered
in the presence of:

_____   _____
            Witness   Signature of officer

                                       _____
                                              name of company

_____   By _____
            Witness   name and title of officer

STATE OF_____)
) SS.
COUNTY OF_____)

On this the _____ day of _____, 19__, before me,
_____, the undersigned officer personally
appeared, known to me (or satisfactorily proven) to be the person
whose name is subscribed to the within instrument and acknowledged
that he executed the same for the purpose therein contained.

In Witness Whereof, I hereunto set my hand and official seal.

_____
Notary Public

- This is the general contents of the form many towns and cities use. Be sure to check with your local municipality as to the exact language they require.

RETAIL SECURITY SERVICES
MISSION STATEMENT

RCS exists to provide superior performance to its clients, who are retail merchants of all sizes, in the area of recommending and installing store security systems and procedures. We recognize that our profits and growth are based on the integrity of our dealings and relationships with our clients.

Superior performance means:

- We will deliver quality service and products to our customers' specifications.

- Our dealings with our clients and suppliers will be marked by dignity, fairness and respect.

- We will maintain high levels of productivity and efficiency and constantly strive to improve our product.

- We will continuously reinvest in the business to maintain and improve our ability to keep our clients' stores and employees safe and secure, and to insure that the business has longevity.

- We will be honest, open and respectful to our employees and will encourage mutual concern for health, safety, productivity and accomplishment.

- This mission statement supplies answers to the four key questions: (1) What business am I in (retail security consulting/installation), (2) How should it be conducted (honestly, openly, with mutual respect for clients, suppliers, and employees), (3) What gives me a competitive advantage (superior performance), and (4) What values guide my actions (a desire to succeed and to remain in the business).

MISSION STATEMENT WORKSHEET

What business am I in? Will my clients, employees, and suppliers understand what I am and what I do?

_____
_____
_____
_____
_____
_____

How should my business be conducted? What is important to me, my clients, my employees? What are my standards?

_____
_____
_____
_____
_____
_____

What gives me a competitive advantage? What distinguishes me from my competitors?

_____
_____
_____
_____
_____
_____

What values guide my actions? What will help me stay in this business?

_____
_____
_____
_____
_____
_____
_____

• Your answers to these questions will help you establish direction and strategy. Take the time you need to complete the questionnaire carefully and thoughtfully.

BUSINESS PLAN OUTLINE

1. Executive summary
What is the purpose of the business plan?
What objectives do you plan to meet?

2. Company history
When did/will your business open?
What form of business have you established: sole proprietorship, partnership, corporation?
How long have you or other members of your company been developing or providing this product or service (including prior to joining the company)?

3. Business summary
What business are you in?
What service or product do you provide?
What does your product or service do for your customers? What value/benefit does it have for them?
In what ways is your product or service unique or different?

3. Market
Are you in a stable, growing or declining industry?
Is anything happening or expected to happen in the future that will have a negative (or positive) effect on your business?
Who are your current and/or potential customers?
Who makes the purchasing decisions?
Does your product or service have local, regional or national appeal?
What is the estimated total market in dollars?
What is the current size of the market segment in which you will compete? What percentage do you want or need?

4. Competition
Who are your major competitors?
Describe your competition within your designated geographical

area and within your industry niche. What makes you better than
they are?

How strong is your competition? What is their estimated
annual sales volume? Their share of the market? Is their
business: steady, increasing, or decreasing? Why?

How do your competitors' services or products rate in
comparison to yours? What are their strengths or weaknesses?

What are your strengths and weaknesses in sales or marketing? Production? Supply? Technical expertise? Other
areas?

5. Marketing Plan

By what methods will you sell your product or service?

What price do you anticipate asking for your services?

Is your pricing competitive? Why would someone be willing to
pay your prices?

What are the key components of your marketing and
advertising plan?

6. Management

What is your business background? What management
experience have you had? What education have you had?

What related work experience do you have in this type of
business that might help you to succeed in this venture?

What resources are available to you if you need additional
assistance? Do you have ready access to an accountant, a
banker, a financial advisor, an attorney, an insurance
agent, office support personnel, and other individuals you
may need to help you with the business?

When will you need to hire additional personnel? What will
their jobs be and how much will you need to pay them?

What will your starting salary be? Within two years?

7. Financial information

What do your sales and expenses look like for the first five
years of the business?

- You can rearrange and combine categories to form a logical presentation appropriate to
your business and your market.

- Review your plan with your financial advisor as you prepare it. The input can be very
important in developing a thoughtful, comprehensive plan.

Business Plan for

POWER COMMUNICATIONS, INC.
A consulting/seminar company
created for improving communication skills

EXECUTIVE SUMMARY

This plan details the need for writing/communication skill training in the nation's workforce, and describes how we will satisfy that need. Our system of instruction, called THE WRITE WAY, will:

1. introduce the company into the marketplace
2. offer back-end materials to enhance revenue from seminars
3. publicize our name for more general consulting work

The seminars will be sold via direct response, telemarketing and direct contact with company principals. It is anticipated that we will generate no less than $150,000 in revenues in the first year of operations (on a $20,000 investment), and add at least $150,000 per year for each of the following four years.

COMPANY HISTORY

The company was incorporated on January 10, 19XX in the State of Delaware. The principals are Gerald R. Corliss and Paul Reston (see details in MANAGEMENT section). Both principals have extensive backgrounds in the training and development field, and have pooled their knowledge to create unique testing and follow-up workshops/seminars, based on the test results. Additional materials have also been developed, for sale during and after the seminars.

While they have been creating the materials and methods that will form the base of Power Communications, Inc., the principals have been conducting consulting work with organizations such as Lemon Industries and Barcus Barbecue Grills. These companies and several others will be the first clients of the new business.

BUSINESS SUMMARY

The national media has begun to report on what the principals have been telling corporate and government human resource personnel for years: that many employees—even bright employees with advanced degrees—cannot write well, and fail to communicate even simple thoughts. The cost of miscommunication and lost productivity is calculated to be in the billions of dollars.

A business administration survey released by the University of Michigan revealed that:

- Over 90% of surveyed managers expressed concern and frustration with the written communication process.
- Fully 40% of today's college graduates have difficulty expressing themselves either orally or in written form.
- Executives spend approximately 70% of their time communicating—either orally or in writing.

In the last several years, a number of consulting organizations have been created to present training seminars for business, industry and government. However, the quality of instruction has varied widely, and the methods used to identify need and level of required intervention have been primitive.

Power Communications, Inc. (PCI) has created:

1. A series of unique tests to identify specific problems in employee writing. No-fee testing will be used to obtain sales.
2. A flexible seminar program designed to address only those areas that require remediation. Traditional seminars force people to sit through comprehensive courses, no matter what their specific needs may be. PCI's program will help reduce training costs because employees will not be subject to overly long, boring sessions during which they lose interest. The program will find acceptance with employers since it will minimize time away from the job. Seminar fees will be approximately $3,500 per class of 20.
3. A two-cassette and workbook follow-up program which can be sold to individuals and corporations for brush-up work. Cost will be $39.95 per student.

4. A train-the-trainer program ($750 per person) that will teach business, industry and government trainers how to conduct the course, helping to gain widespread use of our system. Trainers will purchase PCI's workbooks at $17.50 each, and will pay an annual license fee of $1,000 for the right to teach the course.

   PCI's product is unique because:
   - It allows for customized seminars to meet specific needs.
   - It provides a consistency of training for every company location; everyone uses the same workbook, and all trainers must be certified by PCI.
   - It is based on the work of two well-known, successful business writing consultants/trainers.
   - It is less expensive than traditional classroom training or outside seminars.
   - It offers additional materials that are significant revenue producers.

   This plan will demonstrate how THE WRITE WAY can be profitably marketed to the training market and professional associations.

MARKET

   The training market for business, industry and government has been estimated by various trade journals as being somewhere between two and five billion dollars.

   Virtually every medium-to-large corporation has a training or human resource department. There is a major professional association—the American Society for Training and Development—with more than 40,000 members. It is estimated that there are at least another 40,000-60,000 trainers who are not members. Trainers purchase products and services for tens of millions of employees.

In addition to this primary market, there is a strong secondary market: white collar personnel who are members of professional associations. Although not as seminar-intensive as the training market, there are approximately 15 large associations—with three million members—who can purchase our service.

Target Market
(1)   Training Marketplace
Trainers, Business and Industry 35,830
Trainers, Government/Military 6,580
Medical Institutions 4,050
Educational Institutions 7,022
Public/Corporate Libraries 8,320
Corp. Execs 10,282
                              TOTAL 72,084

(2)   Professional Marketplace
15 Professional Societies
(ABA, AMA, ADA, AIAA, ASME,
ASCE, ACS, AIChE, IMA, AICPA,
AHA, ANA, NMA, ASM, DPMA) representing 3.2MM members.

COMPETITION
Local training consultants who purport to be experts in business writing provide theoretical competition. However, their courses are narrow, and they do not have the authority of a national organization. Plus, most do not have testing capabilities or follow-up materials.
More serious competition is found in two independent study courses, THE POWER OF BUSINESS WRITING and WRITE IT DOWN. While not seminar programs, they siphon off training funds that could be invested in seminar programs.
(1) THE POWER OF BUSINESS WRITING is a good product. It has not had a revision in eight years, however. Even though the techniques are still valid, the course appears to be dated. The product, which has three workbooks, three paperback books, and

six audiocassettes, sells for $179.95, comparing favorably to our average per pupil cost. It appears, however, that the product contains too much material. According to a group of trainers, employees balk at completing so much work. They want something that is less academic. Sales of this product have never exceeded 7,000 units in any one year.

(2) WRITE IT DOWN! ($125.00) is more motivation than writing instruction. The accompanying videocassette is well produced and full of wit. It is entertaining and trainers buy it because they feel that employees will respond to it. The main criticism, however, is that the course helps people understand and recognize what good writing is...but it doesn't help them learn how to do it. It's the opposite end of the spectrum from THE POWER OF BUSINESS WRITING.

Distribution/Sales Strategy

Sales to the training market will be approached as follows:
- Direct Mail to training universe (3x per year)
- Self-issued public relations
- Telemarketing (largely follow-up to leads)
- Personal visitations
- Will explore possibility of using commissioned reps (this will be a second-year activity).

Success Potential

(1) Lack of competition. Most training consultants make their income by consulting with an organization, then adding a seminar component, when possible. We are creating a national network of associates to provide training throughout the country. While there are several national seminar organizations, but they run open programs in meeting halls; they do not customize course material to suit in-house programs.

(2) Convenience and consistency. With an extensive network of associate trainers, as well as certified in-house trainers, seminars can be delivered in virtually any location without significant set-up expense. And the training is consistent for employees throughout the country. Follow-up tape materials continue the consistency of approach.

(3) Price. Most classroom writing programs start at $300-$400 per person. THE WRITE WAY costs $175 per person and, with frequency discounts, can cost as little as $135.

(4) Value. Most seminars use a nondescript three-ring binder filled with hand-out sheets. THE WRITE WAY offers a professionally-published workbook that has "keepability." There is a perception of enhanced value with the books, as well as the fact that employees will take a course tailored to their specific needs.

MANAGEMENT

Gerald R. Corliss, president of PCI, is a specialist in instructional design who has directed the development of such well-known corporate courses as Understanding the Communication Flow, Writing for Business, and Management Negotiating.

Mr. Corliss has authored and edited communication programs used in adult education programs nationwide through the Lincoln Foundation and the University of Minnesota, for whom he also edited and designed management research surveys and personal assessment systems. He has conducted experimental methods of instruction for the United States Army and has spent his entire career in the training, development and instruction of communication-based programs. He has trained employees at all levels for companies such as KMI, United Chassis, and J&G Pharmaceuticals.

Mr. Corliss is a member of the American Society for Training and Development and the National Society for Performance and Instruction.

References

Laura Blaylock, Director of Human Resource Management, KMI Corp., 1 White Horse Park, Chicago, IL 60606, 312-555-9909.

William Moore, VP Personnel, United Chassis, 401 N. Broad Street, Detroit, MI 48242, 313-555-6600, ext. 2424.

Ellen Arons, Training Coordinator, J&G Pharmaceuticals, Executive Campus West, Flint, MI 48507, 313-555-9876.

Paul Reston, executive vice president of PCI, has developed more than 40 training products, in many formats, including interactive audio and video, software, and print. He has specialized in communication skill training, creating courses for improving speech, conversation, reading, writing, listening, and thinking.

Mr. Reston has spoken on communication skills throughout the world, and has written columns and articles on communication skills for national publications, including Training Motivation and Management, and Adult Educator.

Mr. Reston also has considerable marketing skills, having created licensing deals for training programs with organizations such as Cannard Steel, Washington Pipeline, and Robertson Heating Products.

He has been an officer in the American Society of Training and Development, and is a member of the American Marketing Association.

References
Leonard Michaels, Vice President Operations, Cannard Steel, 1200 Carnegie Place, Pittsburgh, PA 15227, 412-555-8900.

Cornelius Macklin, Vice President Human Resources, Washington Pipeline, 2400 David Place, Bellevue, WA 98004, 206-555-0202.

Sharon Haines, Communication Training Specialist, Robertson Heating Products, 100 Progress Plaza, Dayton, OH 45402, 513-555-1818.

Salary Schedules
At this time, only Mr. Corliss and Mr. Reston are working for the company. It is not anticipated that additional management personnel will be required until the third year. Salaries will be $30,000 each in the first year, and $60,000 each in the second year (both years represent about 1/3rd of projected income). If sales exceed anticipated levels in the second year, bonuses may be issued, not to exceed 15% of pre-tax profits.

Mr. Corliss and Mr. Reston are 50-50 partners in this venture. Both will forego company benefits for the first two years.

FINANCIAL INFORMATION

<u>Sales Forecast</u>
      1st year:
35 classes @ $3,500 ea $122,500
10 train-the-trainer programs @ $750
   per person/4 people per class 30,000
10 licenses @ $1,000 ea   10,000
200 additional workbooks @ $17.50 ea 3,500
200 audio kits @ $39.95 ea .... <u>7,990</u>

                          TOTAL $173,990

      2nd year:
70 classes @ $3,500 ea $245,000
25 train-the-trainer programs @ $750
   per person/4 people per class 75,000
25 licenses @ $1,000 ea 25,000
500 additional workbooks @ $17.50 ea 8,750
500 audio kits @ $39.95 ea .... <u>19,975</u>

                          TOTAL $373,725

Profit Analysis-First Year
Seminars
10 trainers (20 days @ $60/day) $12,000
typeset/print 1,000 workbooks 3,800
narrate/duplicate 500 sets of tapes 2,200

Marketing
direct mail 40,000
telemarketing 10,000
travel/entertainment 6,000

Office
rent 18,000
staff salary..18,000
supplies.. 8,000
principal salaries...60,000

TOTAL $178,000

The first year is basically break-even. The second year antici-
pates a modest increase in costs to reflect the need for more
materials and outside trainers. Principal salaries will double to
reflect more realistic compensation. If sales goals are attained in
the second year, bonuses will be awarded.

Operating Income/(Loss)

Estimated five-year sales volume and expenses follow:

(In thousands)

	Year 1	Year 2	Year 3	Year 4	Year 5
SALES	$ 174	$ 374	$ 530	$ 690	$ 850
COST OF GOODS SOLD					
Materials & Trainers	18	34	60	90	120
Staff Salaries	18	20	38	60	65
Total Cost of Goods Sold	36	54	98	150	185
GROSS PROFIT	138	320	432	540	665
OPERATING EXPENSES					
Direct Mail	40	50	60	70	80
Telemarketing	10	25	45	65	70
Commissioned Reps	—	10	25	35	45
T&E	6	10	14	19	25
Rent	18	20	22	28	30
Office Supplies/Eqpt	8	10	15	20	24
Officers' Salaries	60	120	150	180	200
TOTAL OPERATING EXP.	142	245	331	417	474
PRE-TAX PROFIT (LOSS)	$ (4)	$ 75	$ 101	$ 123	$ 191

Expense Items
- Outside trainers ($600 per day currently; anticipate 20 days in
  1st year, approximately 2-1/2 times that in subsequent years).
- Workbooks (development $2,000; $1.80 per book for printing).
- Audiotape (development $500; $.85 per tape for duplication).
- All other costs, see P&L.

• Use an Executive Summary to prepare readers for what will follow. Include a table of contents if your plan is more than a few pages long.

• If you're seeking funds, your financial section needs to be fleshed out, fully examining expenditures on a year-by-year, item-by-item basis. The use of a knowledgeable financial advisor is strongly suggested.

Setting Your Fees 3

All consulting activities should have a specified fee, to be defined clearly at the beginning of a project, either in a formal contract or letter of agreement. (Sample contracts are found in Chapter 8.) Financial arrangements must be spelled out in a binding document so that there is no confusion or disagreement about the cost of a consultant's services, appropriate billing procedures, and payment terms.

Determining how much to charge for services is often one of the biggest challenges for a new consultant. There are a number of factors to examine before you can feel comfortable answering the inevitable question that prospective clients bring up early in their conversations with you: "How much do you charge?" or "How much will this project cost us?"

Start by examining your costs. Costs can be broken down into direct and indirect expenses. In the simplest terms, a **direct cost** is any expense that is incurred for a specific project or consulting assignment, and is, therefore, billable to the client. An **indirect cost** is any expense that cannot be assigned or traced to a specific project. Indirect expenses, are considered overhead expenses, since they must be absorbed by your consulting practice. A list of Direct Costs (3-01) and Indirect Costs (3-02), found at the end of this chapter, can be used for keeping track of expenses.

Because consulting is a "labor intensive" business (one in which your work time is the major cost), the next step to calculating your fee structure is to factor in the cost of your labor. A good place to start is to use your previous salary. For example, if you were making $50,000 in the corporate world, you might use that figure for your labor cost. You could also use the salary of a comparable position. Regardless of what you choose to use, the figure should reflect what someone with your experience and abilities could earn as an employee.

Both indirect and labor expenses must be converted to a daily figure so that they can be used in calculating your daily rate. Refer to Figure 3a.

PRELIMINARY DAILY RATE CALCULATION

Direct Labor Cost	=	$50,000
Indirect Costs (60% overhead rate)	=	$30,000
Subtotal		$80,000
Daily expenses (Subtotal divided by 260 days)		$308
Profit Estimate (20% of daily expense)	=	$62
Daily rate		$370

Figure 3a

Suppose your labor expense was $50,000 and your overhead (indirect costs) was $30,000. Dividing the total of $80,000 by 260 work days a year (52 weeks x 5 days) equates to a consulting fee of $308 per day. This would cover your labor costs and indirect costs, but would not include even a small allowance for profit.

Incidentally, it's a good idea to calculate your overhead *rate*, to make sure it's not out of the normal range. The overhead rate is the overhead expense divided by the labor expense. While there is no "ideal" overhead rate, a well-managed consulting practice would probably have an overhead rate somewhere in the 60-80% range. In our example, the overhead rate is 60% ($30,000 divided by $50,000).

In order for your business to be successful, you should be earning a profit over and above your labor and overhead expenses. Profit is expressed as a percentage of total costs. While there is no magic number, a range of 15-30% is often used as a benchmark. Returning to our previous example, a 20% profit would bring the daily consulting rate to $370.

Before you begin using the daily rate developed so far, there are a number of very important factors that need to be considered.

ACTUAL BILLING TIME

Days

Number of workdays	260
Time Off	- 32
Administrative (1 day every 2 weeks)	<u>- 26</u>
	202
Business Development (30%)	<u>- 61</u>
Subtotal	141
Downtime (25%)	<u>- 35</u>
Total	106

Figure 3b

You need to ask yourself:

1. How much time off are you planning to take during the year? What about vacation time and allowance for some unplanned time off for illness or personal emergencies?
2. How much time is needed for routine administrative duties or office responsibilities (like bookkeeping, billing and other such activities) that cannot be billed to clients?
3. How much time is needed to develop and expand the business by making marketing calls, visiting prospective clients, making promotional presentations, or performing other business development activities that also cannot be billed to clients?

To show how these factors will affect consulting fees, let's fill in some arbitrary numbers and apply them to our earlier calculations. Refer to Figure 3b. For our purposes, let's assume the following:

- You want to take 12 holidays and 10 vacation days this year, and plan to have a 10-day cushion for any surprises or emergencies.

This will reduce the 260 days by 32.

- You estimate 1 day every two weeks for office time and administrative work. This will reduce the days by another 26.
- You estimate about 30% of your time for various business development activities. This, of course, is based on the "adjusted time" resulting from the two previous decisions.

There is one other variable that needs to be added into the equation. It is very unlikely that you will be able to sell every available billable hour. There will be times when no client has bought your available time. Unsold time (also called non-billable time or downtime) needs to be factored in to your pricing formula.

Most new consultants are encouraged to expect non-billable time in the neighborhood of 25% of available time. Using this estimate, you will need to reduce the daily calculations again, from 141 days to 106 days. Note that this is a safe way to estimate billable time during your first year or so in business. As your client base increases, the number of billable days will increase.

Refer to Figure 3c for the final daily rate calculation.

FINAL DAILY RATE CALCULATION

Direct Labor Cost (Based on annual salary)	=	$50,000
Indirect Costs (60% overhead rate)	=	$30,000
Subtotal		$80,000
Daily expenses (Subtotal divided by 106 days)		$755
Profit Estimate (20% of daily expense)	=	+$151
Total daily rate		$906

Figure 3c

Now that realistic time considerations have been factored in, you can see why fees for an independent consultant may seem high to employees who are paid on a straight salary (plus benefits) basis. There are very few company employees who are making close to the daily rates that this consultant needs to charge.

However, the fees used in these examples are not unusual or extravagant. Although there are no standard rates, a common fee for consultants is between $1,000 and $1,500 per day. And the "first tier" of consultants charge a minimum of $500 *per hour.*

The daily rate fee is the most common of several fee methods used by consultants. Fixed price fees are also used, though somewhat less frequently. A Daily Fee Calculation Worksheet (3-03) and a Fixed Price Fee Calculation Worksheet (3-04) are found later in the chapter. In addition to daily fees and fixed price fees, several other fee arrangements are commonly used. A Description of Fee Types (3-05) is located at the end of the chapter.

Regardless of the method you use to calculate your fees, there are a number of factors that should be considered when deciding how much to charge. Some issues that should affect your decision include:

1. Your reputation in the industry or field of endeavor. This includes academic degrees, publishing credentials, copyrights or patents, and any other distinguishing activity that makes you a recognized expert or authority.

2. The kind of assignment. Gathering information for a client is less significant (and should cost less) than making and implementing a program or resolving an ongoing problem.

3. Your need to establish a relationship with a particular company or develop a reputation within a new industry. Initially, you may not be able to charge new clients what others have been paying you for years.

4. Your own estimate of the value you are bringing to the project.

5. Your sensitivity about the prevailing rate in the industry or marketplace.

6. Your willingness to work with a prospective client who has a limited budget.

DIRECT COSTS
(Expenses directly billable to a client—in addition to your fee)

Transportation (taxis, car rentals, airfare,
    airport shuttles) _____
Hotel and motel expenses _____
Food while traveling (actual costs or
    per diem allowance) _____
Telephone/fax charges (directly related
    to a specific project) _____
Printing/copying of project reports or materials _____
Rental of special equipment _____
Express mail or overnight delivery charges _____
Computer or database usage charges _____
Secretarial or administrative support
    required for specific project _____
Other _____ _____
Other _____ _____
Other _____ _____

- Identifying all direct costs prevents you from shortchanging yourself on expenses for which the client should rightfully be billed.

- Make sure these expenses are specified in the contract, to avoid conflict later.

INDIRECT COSTS
(General overhead expenses not directly billable to clients)

Office rent	_____
Utilities	_____
Insurance (medical, life, disability)	_____
Local, state and federal taxes	_____
Office equipment (computer, copier, fax machine)	_____
Telephone equipment and service	_____
Marketing and promotion costs	_____
Printing and copying	_____
Office supplies	_____
General postage and mail expenses	_____
Automobile lease	_____
Automobile repairs and gas	_____
Dues to professional associations	_____
Entertainment	_____
Accounting or bookkeeping fees	_____
Legal fees	_____
Other _____	_____
Other _____	_____
Other _____	_____

- Identifying and tracking indirect costs is an important step in controlling your business, and prevents unwelcome surprises.

Daily Fee Calculation Worksheet (3-03)

DAILY FEE CALCULATION WORKSHEET

Direct labor cost (annual requirement)	=	$_____
Overhead %	=	$_____
Profit %	=	$_____
Total Gross Annual Income Required	=	$_____

Total number of work days (52 x 5)   260
Time off—number of days per year   - _____
Administrative work—number of days per year   - _____

Total   _____

Business development (____% of Total)   - _____

Available Billable Days   _____

Total Gross Annual Income Required   = $_____

(divided by)   Available Billable Days   = $_____

(equals)   Your Daily Rate   = $_____

• As your administrative and business development time allocations change, revise your worksheet to reflect your recalculated billable days. If it shows the need for a higher rate, use this new rate for new clients, and keep old clients at the original rate until it seems prudent to raise the rate to those clients. Of course, you will want to give them ample warning.

FIXED PRICE FEE CALCULATION WORKSHEET

Example:
For a particular project, the consultant estimates 15 days of consulting time. He currently charges $1,000 per day, and estimates expenses will be $6,000.

Estimated Consulting Fees	=	$15,000
Estimated Expenses	=	$6,000
Sub total		$21,000
Cushion (15%)		$3,000
Grand total		$24,000

Your calculations:

Estimated Consulting Fees	$_____
Estimated Expenses	$_____
Sub total	$_____
Cushion	$_____
Grand total	$_____

• For some projects, it's wiser to establish a fixed price, than to have to explain billing specifics to the client (i.e. having to defend the number of consulting days involved).

• Don't forget to cover possible contingencies in the "Cushion" calculation. This one item could save the project from being a losing proposition for you.

TYPES OF FEES

Daily rate

This is used as the basis for estimating costs for an entire project or consulting activity. For example, a consultant's fee is $900 per day, which is also called a "per-diem" cost or billing rate. If the project will take 10 days to complete, the consultant's estimate for consulting would be $9,000. The billable (direct) costs of any expenses incurred would be added to that total to arrive at a project cost.

Hourly rate

This is a far less common fee structure than a daily rate. Usually, a minimum number of hours is set by the consultant, and travel time is frequently billed by the hour.

Fixed price

This arrangement is based on estimates made by the consultant prior to the start of a particular project. Often, the estimate is an educated guess about the length of time required to complete a particular assignment, plus costs known at the time. Frequently, the estimate is then adjusted or cushioned to allow for errors or surprises. This variation of the daily rate fee structure allows the consultant to refrain from discussing a specific daily rate which might seem excessively high to a prospective client.

A fixed price fee is also used when a consultant simply charges what he thinks the project should be worth to the client.

Fixed price fees can prove problematic for a consultant, since all costs might not be known up front, which could leave the consultant at considerable risk.

Contingency fee

This is a fixed price fee which a company agrees to pay the consultant only if certain results are achieved. This arrangement is usually limited to certain types of consulting—executive recruiting, for example.

Retainer fee

This a fixed-fee arrangement in which the consultant receives regular payments (usually monthly) for time that has been reserved for the client, even if the consultant is not asked by the client to do work. This type of arrangement assures the client that the consultant will be available, if needed.

Charging a retainer fee is a customary practice when there is a long-term, ongoing relationship between a consultant and a client. A retainer simplifies the consultant's invoicing process and the company's payment procedures.

Percentage fee (also called an equity fee)

This is a "cut of the action" in which a client and a consultant agree prior to the start of a project that a portion of the financial outcome will be paid to the consultant. This type of arrangement is most common with sales or marketing projects in which a sales increase is used as the basis for calculating the percentage. Another common application is when a company agrees to pay a percentage of money saved during a specified period of time because a consultant has helped reduce the company's expenses. This fee structure has a number of inherent problems and is not widely favored in the consulting profession.

- While there are a number of methods for calculating fees, daily rate and fixed price are by far the most common.

- It's not a good idea to switch from one type of fee to another with a particular client, unless a specific kind of project clearly warrants it. Clients like to work with a consultant on a fee basis that they expect will continue.

Marketing— Direct Methods 4

It doesn't matter how much you have to offer if prospective clients don't know you exist. It's essential that your message reaches your prospects, or you won't turn them into clients. And without clients, of course, you won't have a business.

Your business plan (see Chapter 3) should include most, if not all, of the following methods of generating clients. This chapter will show you how to implement these techniques.

1. Telemarketing
2. Direct mail
3. Magazine and newspaper advertising
4. Directory advertising
5. Networking

Telemarketing

Anyone who has ever received a phone solicitation knows first-hand how difficult it can be to put the caller off. That's one of the advantages of telemarketing: Because it's a one-on-one encounter, many people will allow the caller to explain the purpose of the call. And most will listen to the caller if they find the topic of interest.

While the best use of the phone is in servicing and reselling existing accounts, you can also make it work for you when you're starting your business by making "cold" calls. These are calls to people you don't know, but whom you think should be good prospects.

One very successful consultant built his practice by making nearly 1,000 cold calls during his first six months in business. If he couldn't get to the person he wanted (often he'd ask for a title; occasionally he had a specific name), he'd talk to a secretary or assistant.

His goal was to get information. If he could learn what the company was doing, he could set up a meeting to explain how he could help the company achieve its goals. And he followed up every opportunity. No job was too small or unimportant, because he knew that a small job could lead to a larger one.

Cold calling success is a question of mathematics. If you make 30 calls a week and receive work from just one of the 30, is it worth your time? Chances are, it is...and if that one account becomes a steady account, it is *well* worth your time.

Here are some tips for cold calling:

1. Write out your script beforehand, and make it conversational. Think about how you would speak to the prospect if you were face-to-face.
2. Get right to the benefits. Tell the prospect how they can enhance profits, productivity, etc.
3. Mention other companies for whom you've achieved similar results.
4. Keep your goal in mind. Realistically speaking, the chances are slim that you'll make a sale on a cold call. Your goal is to get a meeting where you can really sell yourself—and have a chance to offer a proposal.
5. Don't give up if you can't get through to your primary target. In many cases, a prospect's secretary will give you more information about what is going on than the boss will. Use that information to shape a good letter (written material almost always gets through the secretary's defenses).
6. If you feel it is critical that you get directly to the boss with your call, try a few proven tactics:

   • Ask for the boss as if you know him or her. Don't be timid. Obtain the boss's name beforehand. Asking for "the president" or "the director of personnel" is akin to admitting you don't have the vaguest idea who that person is.
   • The boss is usually in the office before and after the secretary/assistant. If you call during off-hours, you'll have a much better chance of the prospect answering the phone. Many large companies have direct dial numbers; simply ask the receptionist for the one you need.

- Send a letter in advance of your call. If you have a particularly well-written, curiosity-arousing letter, it will help pave the way for getting through to the person you're calling. But even if you don't, by sending a letter prior to your call, you can always tell a protective secretary (if you're asked) that the purpose of the call is to review your letter. There's an assumption of prior business, and your call may be put through.

7. Use one of the many sources of names. Some easy-to-obtain resources include:
   - Membership directories of fraternal and other business-related organizations. In some cases, only members are permitted to acquire these resources, so you may have to join the sponsoring organizations to get the listings.
   - Local and state Chamber of Commerce directories provide a "Who's Who" of member companies and key personnel.
   - Directories of professional associations. Most include breakdowns by types of business, as well as phone numbers and individual names.
   - Local and regional phone directories. Businesses are divided by category or specialty, and listings include addresses and phone numbers.
   - Many mailing lists (see Direct Mail below) can now be rented with phone numbers. You can mail a letter or brochure, and then follow up with a phone call.

A Telemarketing Checklist (4-01) and several telemarketing scripts (4-02 through 4-06) and follow-up letters (4-07 through 4-09) are found at the end of the chapter.

Direct Mail

Although direct mail can be expensive, it offers many advantages to the consultant:

- It is totally flexible in terms of how much you mail and when.
- You can easily coordinate your mailing with a follow-up phone campaign.
- You can "test" different approaches. Don't assume that the first letter or mailing package you create is the best one to use. Direct mail professionals agree that even a small change in the opening

paragraph of a sales letter can mean the difference between the success and failure of a promotion.

- You can segment your market to reach only those companies that have the characteristics you're looking for (by numbers of employees, sales dollars, industry, etc.).
- You can personalize your message. Although it's costlier than just sending a form letter, personalizing can pay big dividends. Many secretaries, for example, are instructed to screen bulk ("junk") mail, but a personalized first class letter will be passed along to the boss.

What should you put in your mailing package? Many direct marketing consultants will tell you—particularly when you're starting a new business—to "give it everything you've got." In other words, put your strongest, most effective effort in your first mailing.

By concentrating on putting out a complete promotion—including a letter, brochure and reply card—you'll find out quickly if your market will respond to you and your service. If the mailing is successful in terms of response, then you can test ways of reducing expenses for subsequent mailings (e.g., will the letter and reply card generate sufficient response without the expensive brochure?)

When developing a direct mail promotion, there are certain guidelines that will help your mailing piece achieve success:

1. **Use testimonials**. People are very interested in what their peers have to say. Although you probably won't have any testimonials from your new business, use testimonials from clients in your old business. If you don't have anything in writing from your old clients, don't be afraid to ask them to give you a testimonial now.

   But be careful about using testimonials, no matter how friendly you may be with clients. Ask that they sign a Testimonial Release (4-02) found later in this chapter. Do *not* use testimonials without having a signed release.

2. **Be specific**. Be clear about what you do and what business you're trying to attract. It's okay to be a generalist in your consulting practice, but if you're sending a mailing to engineering firms, your cover letter should certainly deal with your engineering credentials. Create different letters for different markets; it's worth the time and effort.

   Don't use ambiguities. Instead of saying you've done work for dozens of related firms, say that you've "accomplished significant cost savings for Drayton & Bennet, created an orientation manual for GSA, Inc. that helped reduce employee turnover," etc. Don't say things such as, "Statistics show..." Instead, say "According to figures released by the American Society of..." You'll increase your credibility by being specific.

3. **Make your mailing easy to read and understand.** Many people put a lot of work into a brochure, but don't pay enough attention to the cover letter. Remember that the cover letter is usually the first thing your prospect looks at. It should have short paragraphs—most people don't like to read large blocks of type.

  The brochure itself should be divided into easily identifiable sections. One section may deal with the background of the company, another may list clients (past and present), another may list the qualifications and biographies of the principals, and still another might highlight benefits (in other words, use selling copy!).

4. **Employ the services of a professional copywriter.** The knowledge and experience a professional has is well worth the money they will charge to prepare the copy.

5. **Keep aesthetics in mind.** You can bring an appearance of quality to your mailing by upgrading the paper stock. A linen-weave finish, for example, will give a letter a sense of dignity and permanence. A brochure on a rich card stock is something prospects may keep, whereas a brochure on inexpensive offset paper has the look of a throw-away. As with the advice for hiring a copywriter, it's a wise investment to work with a designer on your initial mailings. They will provide the professional image which will impress prospects and bring you business.

6. **Put a business reply card in your mailing.** This makes it clear that you're looking for a response. Be clear about what will happen if the prospect returns the card. For example, will they receive a phone call? Additional literature? A visit?

  Determine what information you want the prospect to supply on the business reply card—but keep in mind that the more information you request, the less likely your chance of receiving a response. For example, if it's critically important that you know the size of the company, the title of the respondent, etc., then by all means ask for it. But if that information can wait until a visit or follow-up call, you're better off not asking for it on the reply card.

  Be sure you make your reply card postage-paid. Many people

will not take the trouble to get a stamp, but they will drop a pre-paid card or envelope into the mail. Contact your local post office for information on obtaining a first-class business reply indicia.

7. **Track responses**. The way to know whether a particular mailing is doing well—down to the specific lists used—is to "key" each list. Keying means that the reply card should contain a number which lets you determine the source of the response. Each mailing list used should have its own unique key number. It can be printed anywhere on the card (or on the mailing label if you use adhesive backed labels, in which case you can ask the respondent to pull it off the outer envelope and put it on the back of his card). Then you can simply sort the reply cards by key number to determine how effective each list was—as well as how the overall mailing performed.

8. **Use the right mailing list.** You can spend as much money as you like on your mailing piece, but if you don't mail it to the right people you might as well not send it at all. Direct marketing professionals know that using the right mailing list is the single most important part of any mailing. A mediocre mailing to a good list is far more effective than a wonderful mailing piece to the wrong list.

   Even experienced direct mail people often use list profes-sionals—list brokers—to make the selection for them. That's because the brokers know what lists provide good responses for a particular kind of product or service. It doesn't cost you a penny more to use a list broker since the list broker is paid by the list owner.

Sales letters (4-10 through 4-25), brochures (4-26 through 4-30), and brochure cover letters (4-31 through 4-35) appear at the end of the chapter.

Magazine and Newspaper Advertising

This is an area that has long been neglected by consultants. Some consult-ants feel that a "professional" shouldn't advertise, but that mindset is disappear-ing as younger practitioners enter the field.

Sometimes the constraints against advertising are financial. It is relatively expensive to advertise in magazines and newspapers, and people are unsure how to measure effectiveness. The famed retailer, John Wanamaker, once said, "I know that 50% of my advertising is wasted. I just don't know which 50% it is."

What follows is a summary of what good advertising should do—and how to be sure your advertising does it.

1. **Explain your product or service.** How can potential clients know what you can do for them unless you tell them? An ad that says, for example, "Harris & Barnes, Management Consultants," along with a name, address, and phone number, isn't saying much.

    Adding a few lines such as "Information Systems...Strategic Planning...Plant Layout and Productivity" helps a reader focus on areas of expertise that help you stand apart from others.

2. **Sell your firm.** In addition to explaining the kind of consulting you do, mention how customers benefit from your services...by saving money, reducing staff, bringing new products on line faster, etc. Client listings are very impressive to prospects, and so are testimonials.

    As with direct mail, make your advertising dollars work best for you by hiring a professional copywriter and designer, perhaps trading services if dollars are tight.

3. **Use the correct media.** Selecting the right publication for your advertising message is critical. The Standard Rate & Data Service (SRDS) publishes reference books that will allow you to determine audience, circulation, cost and other key information. Larger libraries' reference departments will have *SRDS Business Publications*, *SRDS Consumer Publications*, *SRDS Newspapers*, *SRDS Spot Radio and Television*. These are invaluable sources for media selection.

4. **Be measurable.** Once you've created the ad, it's important to determine if it's doing a good job for you. Keep track of responses to determine how well the ad "paid off." To do this, each ad should have its own key number (see #7 in Direct Mail above). You can place a unique "Department #" in your address in the coupon as the key number, or place it in the corner of your coupon. You can also use a phone extension number as a key number.

    It's hard to base results on a single ad. Advertising results tend to build over time. A rule of thumb is to give an ad three chances in relatively rapid succession (e.g., three straight issues of a publication), to allow the reader to become familiar with your name. This also lets you take advantage of the fact that most publications offer a discount for placing 3 ads within a one-year period. Also, if your ad includes a coupon, you may qualify for a special mail order rate. This can make a major difference in your costs.

Magazine and newspaper ads (4-36 through 4-39) appear at the end of the chapter.

Directory and Yellow Pages Listings

Directory listings earn mixed reviews from consultants. Some say they pay off, others indicate they're not worth the time it takes to fill out the forms. As a rule, however, you should take a directory listing if it's (a) free, and (b) in a publication that is industry-specific to your activities.

Many business publications run an annual directory or buyer's guide issue, and they're more than happy to print your listing. Don't wait to see if you receive a listing form. Contact the editors of the publications you feel are read by your clients, and ask that you be put on the list for directory issues.

Additional sources can be found in the *Directory of Associations* by Gale Research, available at most libraries. Many associations and organizations produce buyers guides and approved vendor listings for members. Often, a membership will earn you a free listing.

Until you're certain that a particular publication will work for you, you may not want to pay for extras like bold-faced listings, tinted boxes, etc. Take your free listing and see if any activity is generated.

One listing that is important, if only for verifying that you exist, is your local Yellow Pages. Your local Bell affiliate (as opposed to other directories) will list you for free, and offer you paid enhancements. Many consultants report receiving dozens of calls each year from their phone book listing. Even though it costs extra, some consultants feel it's well worth the price to be listed under various consultant categories: management, marketing, business, industrial, etc.

A Yellow Pages display ad may prove worthy of an additional expenditure. A relatively inexpensive one inch ad may dramatically increase response over a simple line listing.

A Yellow Pages ad (4-40) appears at the end of the chapter.

Networking

Most consultants will claim that their practices were built more from networking than from all other forms of marketing combined. One consultant, for example, received a lead from another consultant many years ago...and has done six figure business with that company every year since. And all it cost was a cup of coffee. Networking should include:

- **Former employers**. These are people who can not only give you references, they can give you jobs. In fact, your expertise can be of great value to your previous employers. Stay in touch with them, and be sure to offer them your services.

- **Clients.** The people for whom you do work are usually more than happy to give you leads on who's doing what. Often, they know of needs that will never be advertised. They are also excellent sources of referrals.
- **Family and friends.** Almost anyone who works may know people who need a consultant. When you're starting out, call everyone you can think of and ask for a name or two. One consultant received an appointment with his next door neighbor's company and turned it into a major account. You never know unless you ask.
- **Other consultants.** Many consultants stay in touch with each other through professional organizations or less formal networks. Although consultants in your specific field may be unwilling to pass names on to you, they may be able to use your services on a subcontracting basis. And non-competing consultants may be more than happy to pass your name along to their clients if you offer to do the same for them. There's no reason why you shouldn't call other consultants to suggest such an arrangement.

A Networking Checklist (4-42) is located at the end of the chapter. Also included are a Letter to Client Letter Requesting Referral (4-43) and a Letter Thanking Client for Referral (4-44).

TELEMARKETING CHECKLIST

1. Do you have a clear goal in mind? (get an appointment, send information, etc.) _____

2. Are you able to clearly and quickly state the benefits you offer to the listener? Can you describe your reason for calling and your service in simple terms? _____

3. Are you ready to meet most objections? Have you prepared in advance? _____

4. Does your contact have the power to hire consultants? Don't be afraid to ask! Don't waste time selling to someone who can't buy. _____

5. Can you point out examples of why your service should be chosen over a competitor's? (Do you know who your competitors are? Can you find out if the prospect company is using consultants?) _____

6. Can you state who is using your service or similar services? (Prospects like to know that other companies are using the type of service you offer.) _____

7. What specific conditions exist (e.g., economic conditions, new competition) that make your service attractive? Can you articulate them and point out how your service fits? _____

8. Do you have literature ready for immediate follow-up? _____

9. Do you have a follow-up system in place (e.g., organizer or call-up software) to insure that you don't waste the lead? _____

- Having a system for your telemarketing efforts will provide the most efficient use of your time.

- Avoid trying to close a sale on the phone. Your goal should be to set up an appointment or send literature—and then be sure to follow up.

TESTIMONIAL RELEASE

I acknowledge that the below mentioned quote or excerpts therefrom may be used by _____ in promotions for its services without any consideration payable therefor.

Accepted by _____ Date_____

- Be sure to get a release for any testimonial you publish. This simple form should be adequate for general use. However, it's always a good idea to have your attorney review any legal form used in your practice.

TELEMARKETING SCRIPT, GENERAL

(If you are talking to the decision maker, a prospect with authority to hire you)

Caller: Hello, my name is John Simms. I'm calling to introduce myself and to ask you for a few minutes of your time today.

Briefly, I'm a local consultant with over 10 years of experience in your business. Most of my work has involved important projects that companies like yours have not had the time or the resources to implement. My assignments have ranged in scope from 3 to 10 days and in complexity from a fairly straightforward management assessment to a more detailed quality control audit.

If you're interested, I would like to talk with you in greater detail about how you can use my expertise and experience to help you start or finish any projects that you've been putting off or moving around on your to-do list.

In fact, if you'd be willing to take a few minutes now to describe one of your pressing projects, I'd like to meet with you next week to discuss how I could be a cost-effective resource to help you get the job done. Or, if you'd prefer, we could meet for a few minutes to discuss my background, experience and fees.

Would next Tuesday at 8:30 be convenient for you? Fine, I'll see you then.

(If the prospect resists a meeting)

If you wouldn't mind then, I'd like to send you some

information describing my background and some of the services I can provide, just for future reference in case you have a need for some short-term assistance.

(Call a week later to make sure the prospect has received and understands the information you sent.)

(If screened by the prospect's administrative assistant or secretary—Use introduction and attempt to schedule a later telephone call with the prospect. If that is not possible, state that you will be sending some information about yourself for the prospect to review. Make a note to call again three or four days later, soon after your information should arrive in the mail.)

(If you get an automated message—Most of this script will work to introduce yourself. Then set up a follow-up telephone call to the prospect.)

- Notice that the script does not mention fees. It focuses on your providing help for small, well-defined projects that the prospect has been looking for a way to get done.

- This script is an excellent way for you to "get your foot in the door" of many prospects. It can be tailored easily for almost any consulting service.

TELEMARKETING SCRIPT, IMPORT-EXPORT

Caller: Hello, my name is Bill Wilson, from CLT Limited, a consulting firm specializing in import/export assistance, and I'd like to ask you a question. Do you believe that delays are unavoidable in the shipping business?

(If Prospect answers YES to the question, respond:)

Caller: That's what nearly everyone in your position says...at first. But fifteen years of experience in the import/export business have convinced me that delays really can be avoided.

Here are a couple of questions to prove my point. Have you ever had a shipment delayed because of an overaggressive customs inspector?

Prospect: More times than I care to count.

Caller: And have you ever had to work overtime because a forwarder promised more than he could deliver?

Prospect: Yes.

Caller: I could go on and on, but you've already heard all the excuses.

(If Prospect answers NO to the question about delays, respond:)

Caller: You may have been around as long as I have. But my fifteen years of experience in the import/export business have convinced me that delays <u>can</u> be avoided. Even though there are always going to be overaggressive customs inspectors and forwarders who promise more than they deliver, they're not really the problem.

(Continue with the following in <u>either</u> case:)

Caller: The truth is that virtually all shipping problems are caused by improper documentation. Think about it: It's improper documentation that waves a red flag at customs officials. It's improper documentation that forces shippers to get banks into the act to guarantee freight costs and drive up the price of shipping. It's improper documentation that causes long delays, explanations, and increased costs.

I can help you save as much as 25% of your import/export costs—and dramatically speed up your shipments—by reviewing your documentation procedures and creating guidelines for you and your vendors. All I need is about 30 minutes of your time, and I'll give you an overview of what needs to be done to improve your profitability. What day next week is best for you?

(If the listener doesn't want to set a date, say that you'll send literature that will demonstrate the importance of your service, and that you'll call after the listener has had the opportunity to review the material.)

- Establish your credentials quickly (e.g., "Fifteen years of experience in the import/export business...")

- To get a meeting, explain what's in it for the prospect ("...save as much as 25%...speed up shipments...").

TELEMARKETING SCRIPT, MANAGEMENT TRAINING

Caller: Hello, I'm Mark Engstrom from Ark Training Associates, and I'd like to ask if you feel the quality of the letters, memos and reports written by your staff could stand improvement?

Prospect: Sure.

Caller: Then you'll be interested in the results of a study conducted by IT&C. They wanted to determine what made some managers so much better than other managers. One of the six skills they identified as making top managers stand out was the ability to communicate clearly through the written word.

(Some prospects may want to know the other skills. Tell them you'll give that information in a couple of minutes. That will (a) keep them listening, and (b) prevent from straying from the purpose of your call.)

Caller: I'm one of the two people who helped IT&C install a national writing improvement program after the study was validated. My partner and I have taken the techniques that were so successful for IT&C and combined them into a writing program that will upgrade your employees' writing skills. Do you currently have a writing training program?

(If Prospect answers NO, respond:)

Caller: Conducting a writing seminar will be a terrific way to get more productivity out of your employees. Wait 'til you see the confidence they gain from a writing seminar...and watch how much time is saved when they learn to state their thoughts more quickly and with far greater clarity. No mistakes, no misunderstandings. Just perfect two-way communication every time. I'd like the opportunity to show you why so many corporations and government agencies offer writing programs to their employees.

(If Prospect answers YES, respond:)

Caller: That's wonderful. Your company sounds very progressive. I'd like to discuss the advantages that our writing system offers, including the flexibility of different schedules...the ability to use your own trainer...a built-in correspondence option for employees on the road...and a very low cost.

(Continue with the following in either case:)

Caller: May we meet to review your employees' writing needs?

(If Prospect declines to meet, ask if you may send literature. Then follow up within a week.)

• Questions help focus listeners, as do studies and survey reports from other companies. Use both to gain attention.

• Validate your previous experiences and it won't matter if your company is brand-new. Sell *yourself*.

TELEMARKETING SCRIPT, MARKETING

Caller: Hello, I'm Martin Boyle, and my company is BMA Marketing. We've helped companies dramatically increase their sales through telemarketing. And if you have a moment, I'd like to tell you how I can do the same for your company.

Do you currently have a telemarketing operation?

(If Prospect does not currently use telemarketing, respond:)

Caller: Well, you might want to consider adding one, because many companies who use telemarketing are reaping remarkable benefits.

(If Prospect currently does use telemarketing, respond:)

Caller: That's good news, because the companies who use telemarketing—at least the ones with whom my company works—are reaping remarkable benefits.

(Continue with the following in either case:)

Caller: For example, a local contractor, Ludmiller Brothers—do you know them?

(It doesn't matter if Prospect answers YES or NO, it's important just to keep him involved in your narrative.)

Caller: They've lowered their field selling costs by 38%. Business has never been better for them and they've done it by getting more qualified leads through telemarketing.

Have you heard of the hot new beer—Cantina Beer?

(Again, the answer doesn't matter. Your goal is to keep the Prospect alert and thinking along with you.)

Would you believe they've increased their market share, in only six months, by an amazing 52%? Their president, Will Rodriguez, attributes the gain to constant distributor contact over the phone. And consistently good scripts for their telemarketers.

(If Prospect does not currently use telemarketing, respond:)

Caller: There are many more examples of tremendous growth through telemarketing. May I send you information on how establishing a telemarketing operation in your company can boost your sales or profits? (ALTERNA-TIVE: Would next Tuesday be convenient to discuss how you can use telemarketing to boost your sales and profits?)

(If Prospect currently does use telemarketing, respond:)

Caller: Since you're already using telemarketing, I think you'd be interested in learning how some of our techniques might be of value in enhancing your operation. May I send you information? (ALTERNATIVE: Would next Tuesday be convenient to discuss how our successful telemarketing techniques can further boost your sales and profits?)

- Be prepared for questions that ask *how* these various companies accomplished their achievements...but save most of your information for the face-to-face meeting that you want.

- Remember: you can use previous experience—accomplishments you generated in earlier jobs—in your sales pitch.

Follow-Up Letter, Import-Export (4-07)

Company Name
Address
City, State Zip

Date

Mr. Bert Campion
Spitzer's Gifts
5900 Weller Street
Minneapolis, MN 55477

Dear Mr. Campion:

Shortly after we spoke, one of my colleagues told me about a company that was trying to import a large shipment of portable disc players. The documentation they presented to customs described the material as "electronics." The company didn't know it, but that's the kind of vague description that arouses suspicion not only by customs inspectors, but by U.S. regulatory agencies, as well.

That company spent countless hours reconstructing the paperwork and waiting out lengthy delays as containers were unpacked and searched. All because of a too-general description.

There are countless traps in the export business, Mr. Campion. Thirty minutes of your time may help you avoid virtually all of them. I'll call to confirm an appointment.

Sincerely,

Bill Wilson

• Try to make your examples specific to the industry in which the prospect works.

• Don't use a "far-out" example. Stick to categories that are widely understood.

Company Name
Address
City, State Zip

Date

Ms. Estelle Stanley
Coronado Office Supplies
11 Delaval Place
Mobile, AL 36633

Dear Ms. Stanley:

Thank you for giving me so much time during our phone conversation last Thursday. Since we covered a lot of ground, I thought it might be of value to give you a summary of what you have to gain from our service:

1. Ease of Training: THE WRITE WAY requires only 8 hours of classroom work per employee, which can be led by your own personnel.
2. Low Cost: THE WRITE WAY costs as little as one-quarter the expense of traditional writing seminars.
3. Validated Results: Employees will confidently write memos, letters, and reports that deliver the intended message, and they'll write them in less time.

The enclosed brochure highlights our experience and clients. We can give you the results you want quickly and inexpensively.

I'll call you next week to set up a meeting and show you how cost-effective our programs are.

Sincerely,

Mark Engstrom

- Repetition of the phone script helps reinforce the primary message.

- Be sure to follow up. Do it while the content is fresh in the recipient's mind.

Company
Address
City, State Zip

Date

Mr. Jerry Rohm
Nemeyer Sporting Goods
Fox Chase Shopping Center
Bloomington, IN 47401

Dear Mr. Rohm:

I'm glad we had the chance to talk about expanding your sales through telemarketing. I can show you how numerous retailers—large and small—have created significant new sales with telemarketing...while reducing their selling costs.

The enclosed literature describes some of the case histories we spoke about as well as some of the retailing statistics that are certain to surprise you. In many cases, telemarketing appeals pulled in far more store traffic than expensive advertising.

I'll give you a few days to digest this important material and then I'll call for an appointment. I look forward to showing you how the telephone can become a major part (a highly profitable one!) of your marketing program.

Sincerely,

Martin Boyle

- Remind the prospect that you spoke on the phone.

- Increased sales and profits are the main reasons for a businessperson to see you. Be sure to state that your service will positively impact their company.

Company
Address
City, State Zip

Date

Mr. Daniel Oates
Stillwater Lumber Supply
142 Herndon Avenue
Minot, ND 58702

Dear Mr. Oates:

Here are the three most common ways companies lose thousands of dollars on their computer operation:

1. They use about 5% of their word processing capability. Most companies don't know the simple techniques to create brochures, utilize type to its best advantage and a host of other functions that can save thousands of dollars in outside costs.

2. They waste tremendous amounts of operator time by not knowing how to automate their systems. If, for example, you mail a letter to your clients and prospects each month, you can merge your data base with a standard form letter using just two key strokes.

3. They don't integrate their existing systems. Many companies, for example, have information in their accounting package that can be used by the marketing department, and vice-versa. Companies waste thousands of dollars by not integrating valuable data.

I can help you save many thousands of dollars and increase your efficiency at the same time. I'll call next week to set up a no-obligation discussion about your computer system...and how you can get the most from it.

Sincerely,

Steven Greene

- Use examples that have universal recognition.

- Numbering the items adds visual interest and clarity.

Sales Letter to Prospect, Engineer (4-11)

Company
Address
City, State Zip

Date

Mr. Jules Bregman
McLaughton Aerospace Systems
1200 Worth Avenue
St. Louis, MO 63143

Dear Mr. Bregman:

Have you ever lost a contract because you didn't have someone in your organization with the necessary experience...or watched a contract go to another company because they had better contacts?

Suppose your team included a skilled Systems Engineer and Program Manager with 25 years of experience on many of the world's aerospace and satellite programs. And suppose he had advised governments and businesses in the U.S., Canada, Germany, Japan, France, China, and Israel on the technical/commercial aspects of satellites.

Do you think that person could make a difference in your company? I've recently started my own consulting business and I'd like to put my expertise to work for you. I've enclosed complete background information for your review. I'd like to visit you and your facility to discuss current and future projects.

I'm confident I can increase your contracts. I'll call you next week to set up a meeting.

Sincerely,

Gordon Busch, Ph D.

- If you have extensive industry experience, spell it out. It's important to distinguish yourself from the crowd.

- People always remember "the ones that got away." Use the "problem-solution" approach to get a hearing.

Company
Address
City, State Zip

If you're like a lot of people,
you might be headed for an unhappy
retirement, dramatically underfunded,
forced to cut back on your lifestyle.

Dear Friend:

You might be headed for trouble. It could be because you think you can continue to work forever. It could be because you vastly underestimate your life expectancy. Or it could be because you're too busy worrying about the here and now to think about what may happen in 10, 15 or 20 years.

Whatever the reason, most people don't think about
their retirement needs until it's too late ...
and when retirement comes,
it's a financial shock and emotional blow.

I can help you beat the statistics that say people 35-44 years old are saving at only one-third the rate necessary to retire at age 65 with no decline in standard of living. I can help you maintain your current standard of living, while insuring that it continues through your retirement.

Call me for a no-obligation discussion of your current and future financial health. Call 617-555-4567 and put yourself in position for financial security...without any strain or difficulty. Act now! While there's still time.

Sincerely,

Jerome Grossman

- Fear is a great motivator for problem-solving.

- You can alter this kind of letter to suit each age group. Substitute the correct statistics, and be sure to send the right letter to the right list!

Sales Letter to Prospect, Management (4-13)

Company Name
Address
City, State Zip

Date

Mr. Abraham Garfinkle
Garfinkle Linen Company
2220 W. Market Street
Birmingham, AL 35203

Dear Mr. Garfinkle:

As the owner of a family business, you may have more than a passing interest in the enclosed article. It could help you avoid one of the primary family business errors. Since you're a busy person, here's a summary of the article:

1. Family businesses usually demonstrate great loyalty to their longstanding attorneys and CPAs. These "advisors" have often been with the business since it began.
2. Quite often, the advisors haven't grown with the business. Many of them stayed small and never gained the required skills to help growing businesses.
3. Many companies have shown dynamic growth by bringing in new advisors who are more attuned to current business practices and techniques.

Your outside advisors should help get you ready for the future. It's no secret that the most prepared organizations are the ones that have the best long-term prospects.

I'd like to meet with you to demonstrate how your advisors can be discretely evaluated...and how much it can mean to you and your company. I'll call within a week.

Sincerely,

George Bixby

- Use related magazine and newspaper articles in your mailings to confirm your claims.

- Highlight key points from the articles to insure that they're read.

Company Name
Address
City, State Zip

Money-Making Idea #8:
Using Notification Mailings
to Generate New Revenues

Dear Association Executive:

As part of your association's membership service, your organization sends various materials to members on a regular basis: notices of new tax laws, medical/insurance coverage and regulations, scientific breakthroughs, conference and meeting dates, membership renewals, and other key data.

Traditionally, notification mailings are thought of as expense items; announcements that must be made, no matter how costly they are. But a few forward thinking associations have learned how to dramatically <u>defray the costs</u> of these mailings. Others have <u>broken even on their costs</u>. And still others have <u>created so much new revenue</u> that they've been able to greatly expand their programs and services. The key is to include promotional offers as "ride-alongs" in the mailings.

If you'd like to generate significant revenues from the mailings you're mandated to make, send the enclosed postage-paid reply card or call us at 1-800-555-9811. We'll give you some ideas that can generate substantial non-dues revenue for you.

Sincerely,

Alan Whittaker

• Be sure you know your audience—and speak their language. Non-profit associations, for example, don't generate "profits," they generate "non-dues revenue."

• Don't date letters that are part of a promotional series. They can be continually reused with new prospects.

Company
Address
City, State Zip

Date

Mr. William Guerin
Ashland Waste Treatment
12 E. Garden View Avenue
Chattanooga, TN 37421

Dear Mr. Guerin:

Do you know why Philadelphia, PA, Fairfax County, VA, Baltimore, MD, and nearly 80% of all medium and large cities and counties have been able to hold the line on taxes? They've privatized many of their services. This trend— contracting with private firms to perform public services—is about to expand into state and federal government, as well.

Wouldn't you like to be in a position to capture
a portion of these booming new revenues?

Various government agencies are looking for firms just like yours. We can guide you through the governmental red tape and put you in touch with the agencies that are actively looking for companies like yours. We can help you contact the right people, complete the right forms, and put you where you need to be to expand your current business through government operations.

Call me at 615-555-0922 or send the enclosed postage-paid reply card to obtain free information on how you can step into the privatization growth market.

Sincerely,

James G. Wellborn

- Cold mailings such as this one can be targeted geographically, by size and type of business, etc., to provide prospects that are likely to be interested in your services.

- Be prepared to follow up in a timely manner while the leads are still "hot."

☐   YES! I want to get my share of privatization dollars.

☐   Send complete information.
☐   Have a representative call for an appointment.

Name _____

Title _____

Company _____

Address _____

City _____ State _____ Zip _____

Daytime Phone # _____

• Repeat your key message on the reply card. It's a strong reinforcement.

• If possible, offer people options for response. It helps get them involved in your services.

Company
Address
City, State Zip

Date

Mr. Alfred Burton
Total Paper Supplies, Inc.
1342 Brick Road
Chicago, IL 60607

Dear Mr. Burton:

Here are a few numbers for you to consider:

18%   22%   31%

Each one represents a gain in market share. The first is the increase I generated as sales manager for Charlton Products (I put their cookware into superstores). The second is the result of my recommendation that Worth Industries acquire a tool and die firm to add specific capabilities. And the third represents the heralded turnaround I helped effect during my tenure at Groton-Pierce (see enclosed article from Industrial Era Magazine).

Now that I've started my own consulting firm, I want to put my track record to work for you. I'd like to have the opportunity to review your business and help you identify strategies that offer the same success ratio I built during my corporate career.

If you want to build increased market share, you'll have the opportunity to start the process when I call next week. I'm looking forward to speaking with you.

Sincerely,

Adam Hunter

- A lack of consulting experience is unimportant in the face of a proven track record.

- Include documentation, such as articles you've written—or that were written about you, that will validate your credentials.

Company
Address
City, State Zip

Discover what Bill Walters'
success strategies can do for you.
Take this opportunity to put
his message to work in your life.
Feel good about your future,
your power, your self-mastery.

Dear Reader:

Don't stop your building process! Turn the momentum and enthusi-asm you possess into a <u>consistent</u> part of your life. Use Bill Walters' Success Conditioning Seminar to build on every taste of success you've had so far. You'll never slide back to unproductive habits...even for a moment!

Let Bill Walters—himself—
disclose powerful new concepts directly to you.

Imagine having the nation's leading success consultant give you new ideas, techniques and get-ahead strategies that will work for you! Imagine learning powerful new techniques that will contribute to improved relationships and emotional and physical well-being month after month, year after year!

Bill Walters' success conditioning helps you understand your <u>basic strengths</u>...learn <u>fundamental truths</u> that apply to your career...realize your <u>goals and ambitions</u>.

Call Toll-Free 1-800-555-8900

Call and reserve your place at Bill Walters' March 16 Success Conditioning Seminar in your city. Attend this meeting and get that special rush of adrenaline that tells you your life will never be the same. Earn the <u>rewards of a lifetime</u> with Bill Walters!

- Match the mailing lists to your message. In this case, rent mailing lists of people who have acquired motivational products or attended motivational seminars.

- Headlines direct the reader to your key message.

Company Name
Address
City, State Zip

Date

Mr. Warren Elision
Hutchings Insurance
5300 W. Billingsley Avenue
Dallas, TX 75370

Dear Mr. Elision:

Last month, one of Dallas' top law firms decided to move their offices to a larger facility. McLintock, Collier & Latham called on us to help plan the move.

Although their new law office was less than half a mile from their former location, the implications of not being ready for business as planned were daunting. In an age of high-tech, instantaneous communication, a move—particularly in a compressed time period—has many complex elements.

The enclosed newspaper article, which is reprinted from last Thursday's Daily News, details how we coordinated movers, furniture and office suppliers, the installation of telephone and fax lines, dedicated computer lines, and other systems and amenities. By 9 am the Monday after the move, the new office was running like clockwork.

More things usually go wrong during a move than go right. If you want them to go 100% right, do what more than 200 firms in Dallas have done in the last 18 months: Call High-Tech Relocation Associates at 1-800-555-6324 to help you plan all the right moves.

Cordially,

Alan Bristow

- Scour news reports about local businesses to trigger prospecting mailings (in this case, articles about companies planning to move).

- Although most publishers are happy to let you reprint articles, get their permission in writing before doing so.

Company Name
Address
City, State Zip

Date

Ms. Elaine Patterson
Midwest Department Stores
1200 North Lane
Waukesha, WI 53151

Dear Ms. Patterson:

Does it surprise you to learn that 72% of all merchandise that's stolen from department stores is taken by employees?

Think about that number for a moment. Of every $100,000 lost to pilferage, $72,000 is taken by workers. That's money that could be used for expansion, upgraded advertising, higher salaries, and other profit-making activities.

Here's what we've uncovered for retailers just like you:

- Employees literally throwing merchandise out windows to waiting accomplices.
- Employees putting half-full boxes out in the trash, then dividing the contents with the haulers after work.
- Employees improperly tagging merchandise so their friends can purchase expensive items at 50%-75% off.

Call 1-800-SECURITY and we'll demonstrate—at no cost or obligation—how we can help you cut employee theft fast, and recapture the profits you deserve. Our short presentation includes actual footage showing how you may be getting ripped off at this very moment...and how you can stop it.

Sincerely,

Barry Murray

- A dramatic opening statement will capture attention.

- Make sure you can back up any statistics you use.

Company
Address
City, State Zip

Date

Mr. Harold Calder
Arrow Knitwear Corp.
Comley and Tacony Streets
St. Louis, MO 63134

Dear Harold:

I think you'll agree that the two people we just acquired for you—
Vice President of Manufacturing and Accounting Supervisor—
have been excellent additions to the firm. I also think our speed in
finding them, and their outstanding qualifications, demonstrate
why we should be working with you on a retainer, rather than a fee
basis.

By engaging us on a job-by-job basis, you pay top dollar. By
switching to a monthly retainer, you'll get the same painstaking
interviewing and evaluation process, but at a third less cost. And
the way your company is growing, there will be many slots to fill.

In addition, Harold, when we're on retainer with a firm, we
consider ourselves part of the firm. We're _always_ on the lookout
for top people for you, not just when you call to fill a slot.

I'll give you a call next week to see if we can get together for
lunch. I'd like to show you how you can upgrade your recruitment
and consulting services at less cost.

Cordially,

Bob Helmer

- It's appropriate to remind your clients that they've received their money's worth from you.

- A recent success provides a good time to suggest to your client that the relationship be moved up a notch.

Company Name
Address
City, State Zip

Date

Mr. Eliot Stanton
President and CEO
Cornell Electric
200 Taylor Ave.
Kansas City, KS 66111

Dear Mr. Stanton:

Great News! As you may have heard, the "Working It Out" seminar we tested with your engineering and operations personnel has been labeled an unqualified success.

In the pilot training session, operations and engineering personnel swapped ideas that, otherwise, might never have seen the light of day. And one suggestion for changing a paperwork procedure has already been adopted...with an estimated savings of nearly $40,000 a year! That's quite a return on your training investment.

Your human resources staff and I want to turn this success into a company-wide commitment, including senior management. If you and your executive staff take the training, it will send a strong message to everyone in the company.

Mary Lake, your human resources director, and I would like to meet with you next week to review the program and anticipated results. To give you a headstart, I've enclosed the results and comments from the pilot program. I hope you'll share our enthusiasm over the benefits this training can bring to Cornell Electric.

Respectfully,

Sharon Anne Waters

- Keeping management in the loop, particularly when there are successes to talk about, helps ensure future projects.

- Aligning yourself with client personnel builds a positive image of someone who is on the company team.

Company
Address
City, State Zip

Date

Mr. Sylvan Kohut
Mercy General Hospital
400 North Broad Street
Washington, DC 20062

Dear Sylvan:

I'm delighted that your corporate management team has enthusi-astically accepted our feasibility study on expansion of the Mercy General facility. And I'm proud that I played a role in such an important project. But before we pop any corks, let me remind you that this is only the first step.

Still ahead for you is the need to sell the expansion to (a) the community, (b) various commissions, and (c) the media. Empha-sis is on the media because once they're convinced, they'll help sell it to the others.

I'd like to be considered part of your "sales" team. As you know, I've been involved with major public relations efforts in the past (see enclosure), and since I know every detail of the expansion study, there's no learning curve; I can get right to work for you.

I'll call you next week to arrange an appointment. And I'll lay out a preliminary plan that can lead to ground breaking within just six months!

Sincerely,

George Foster

- When looking to expand your role in a project, remind the client of your success in the previous phases.

- Point to your familiarity with the project as a stepping stone for getting off to a fast start on the next phase.

Company
Address
City, State Zip

Date

Mr. Arthur Hennessey
Dental Supplies Catalog, Inc.
55 Baltimore Avenue/Suite 301
Augusta, ME 04330

Dear Art:

I think I have an outstanding solution to help you get beyond the 5% annual growth of your catalog. Keep in mind that you've been selling essentially the same products for years, and the audience is shrinking slightly. Actually, we've been fortunate not to have gone backwards. But that won't last forever, given current trends.

Several months ago, I sent a survey to 500 dentists and asked what kind of non-dental products they purchase. And I discovered that we can expand sales by creating a personal development section in your catalog. Instead of just offering drills, picks and other staples, we can offer workout machines, motivational tapes and a number of other items suggested by the research.

Take a look at the enclosed report, and then let's get together to decide how to present this concept to your management. My guess is we can increase sales by at least 20%! Let's go after this new opportunity!

Enthusiastically,

Ross Schafer

- Doing some homework on your own can bring in business—but pick carefully where you spend your time and money.

- Enthusiasm is contagious. Use it to motivate clients and prospects.

Sales Letter to Client, Marketing—Product Development (4-25)

Company
Address
City, State Zip

Date

Ms. Nancy Kuehn
Director of Product Development
JBM, Inc.
2280 50th Court South
Miami, FL 33255

Dear Nancy:

It was a joy working with you on developing the children's Sleepkit. I'm pleased that my research helped us pinpoint such a strong concept. Based on the early sales results you faxed to me, we definitely have a winner!

Since our collaboration proved to be a good one, I've enclosed a few additional ideas for your consideration. They take advantage of what we've learned about the market for very young children, and target many of the same customers for sales. In other words, you'll be able to market these products effectively— and inexpensively—to the same people who buy the Sleepkit.

Incidentally, I've already checked with toy manufacturing sources and packagers. They agree that the enclosed ideas are feasible and easy to mass produce quickly.

Thanks again for selecting me to work with you. I think we can duplicate our success.

Cordially,

Bill Stephan

- Reinforce what went well. Clients often need a "refresher" as to who did what.

- A little preliminary work (e.g., checking sources) can help kickstart a proposed new project.

The brochure (4-26) shown at the right carries the main theme ("Specialists in accounting software technology") through every page. It uses graphics to give what could be a "flat" presentation a compelling appearance.

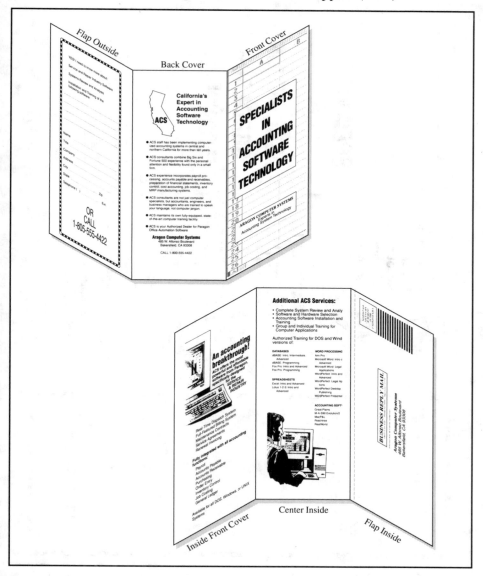

- The six-panel brochure on 8 1/2" x 11" paper or card stock is typically folded into thirds. The top illustration, above, shows the outside "spread" of three panels (including the front and back "covers"). The bottom illustration shows the inside "spread" of three panels. See the following two pages for larger views of the inside and outside panels.

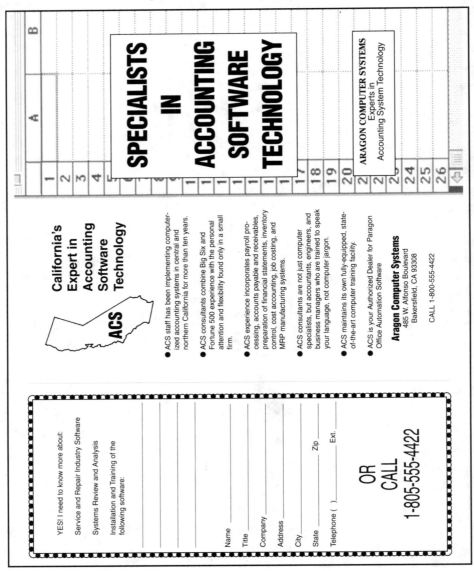

SPECIALISTS IN ACCOUNTING SOFTWARE TECHNOLOGY

ARAGON COMPUTER SYSTEMS
Experts in
Accounting System Technology

California's Expert in Accounting Software Technology

ACS

- ACS staff has been implementing computerized accounting systems in central and northern California for more than ten years.

- ACS consultants combine Big Six and Fortune 500 experience with the personal attention and flexibility found only in a small firm.

- ACS experience incorporates payroll processing, accounts payable and receivables, preparation of financial statements, inventory control, cost accounting, job costing, and MRP manufacturing systems.

- ACS consultants are not just computer specialists, but accountants, engineers, and business managers who are trained to speak your language, not computer jargon.

- ACS maintains its own fully-equipped, state-of-the-art computer training facility.

- ACS is your Authorized Dealer for Paragon Office Automation Software

Aragon Computer Systems
485 W. Alfonso Boulevard
Bakersfield, CA 93308

CALL 1-800-555-4422

YES! I need to know more about:

Service and Repair Industry Software

Systems Review and Analysis

Installation and Training of the following software:

Name _____

Title _____

Company _____

Address _____

City _____

State _____ Zip _____

Telephone ( ) _____ Ext. _____

OR CALL 1-805-555-4422

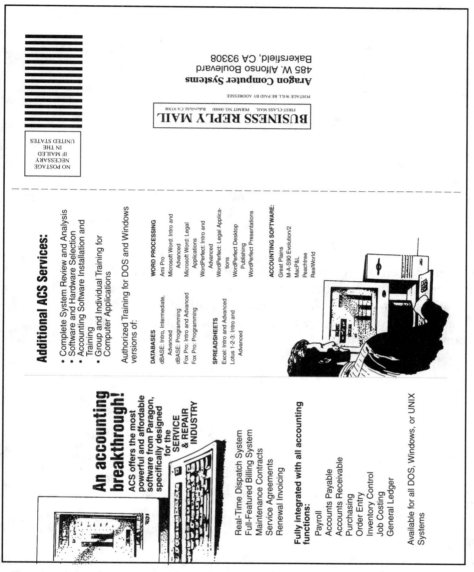

- Target your brochure to a specific market (in this case, the service and repair industry), to get the maximum impact.

- Emphasize your major strength, but list other specialties to attract the widest possible audience.

A letter from the company's principals, along with photos and background information about them, personalize the message in the brochure (4-27) shown at the right. This is an important issue when selling financial services—and other services that require a high level of confidence and trust.

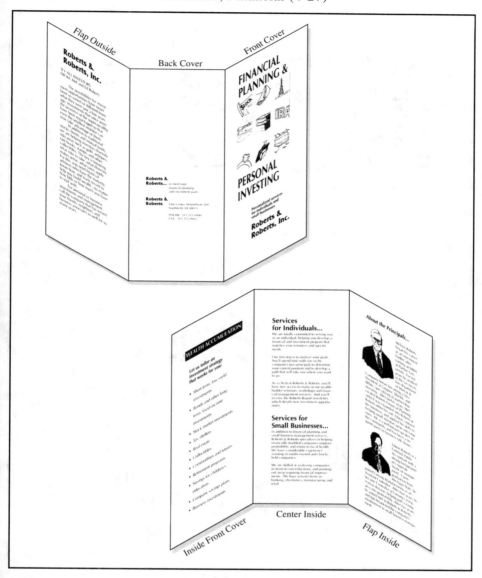

- The six-panel brochure on 8 1/2" x 11" paper or card stock is typically folded into thirds. The top illustration, above, shows the outside "spread" of three panels (including the front and back "covers"). The bottom illustration shows the inside "spread" of three panels. See the following two pages for larger views of the inside and outside panels.

FINANCIAL PLANNING &

PERSONAL INVESTING

Personalized services for individuals and small businesses

Roberts & Roberts, Inc.

Roberts & Roberts... to meet your financial planning and investment goals

Roberts & Roberts One Center Atrium/Suite 201
Southfield, MI 48035

PHONE: 313-555-0900
FAX: 313-555-0902

Roberts & Roberts, Inc.

TO: ALL INVESTORS
FROM: Mel and Ed Roberts

The possibilities for investment opportunities have never been so varied or different from what they were just a few years ago. Investments that once were the province of the super-wealthy have been repackaged so that even the smallest investor can now take advantage of them.

In addition to traditional stocks, bonds and mutual funds, we are helping investors diversify into areas such as gold, antiques, rare books, stamps, and other collectibles. The key is knowing what risks to take, what diversity makes sense, what taxes apply. For this, you need financial advisors who have the maturity, know-how, and track record to help you build wealth...no matter how little or how much you have to start with.

For personal or business investments and management, call the company that has served your friends, neighbors, and business associates so well for so many years.

About the Principals...

Melvyn Roberts began his career as an investment banker after earning an MBA at Purdue University. For ten years he worked in the tax incentive department of Murray & Company before becoming a Vice President at Langtree, Shields, and White, specializing in partnership investing. After twelve years, Mel created Roberts Financial Planning (which was expanded into Roberts & Roberts when his son, Edwin, entered the business), and applied his skills to helping small investors grow into large ones. He is a well-known speaker in the community, and has been a frequent guest on business talk shows.

Edwin Roberts is a Certified Public Accountant with a strong background in corporate financial management. Upon graduation from Michigan State, he joined Lansing Manufacturing as an Assistant Controller. After four years, he became Controller of Lansing's refrigeration division, helping pull a losing area into profitability. After five years, he joined Mel in Roberts & Roberts, and has broadened the company's involvement in small business management.

Services for Individuals...

We are totally committed to serving you as an individual, helping you develop a financial and investment program that matches your resources and specific needs.

Our first step is to analyze your goals. You'll spend time with one of the company's two principals to determine your current position and to develop a path that will take you where you want to go.

As a client of Roberts & Roberts, you'll have free access to many of our wealth-builder seminars, workshops and financial management services. And you'll receive the Roberts Report newsletter, which details new investment opportunities.

Services for Small Businesses...

In addition to financial planning and small business management services, Roberts & Roberts specializes in helping financially troubled companies improve profitability and return to fiscal health. We have considerable experience assisting in family-owned and closely-held companies.

We are skilled at analyzing companies in need of cost reductions, and pointing out areas requiring financial improvements. We have served clients in banking, electronics, manufacturing and retail.

WEALTH ACCUMULATION

Let us tailor an investment strategy that works for you:

- Short-term, low-yield investments
- Bonds and other long-term, fixed-income investments
- Stock market investments
- Tax shelters
- Real estate
- Collectibles
- Commodities and futures
- Retirement programs
- Savings for children's education
- Company savings plans
- Business investments

- Be certain that the front cover highlights your services.

- Listing a *variety* of services (in this case, services for individuals and services for businesses) gives the reader an opportunity to find something that fits their needs.

All elements of the brochure (4-28) shown at the right, from presentation of case histories to the simple description of services offered, make what could be a complex subject easy to understand.

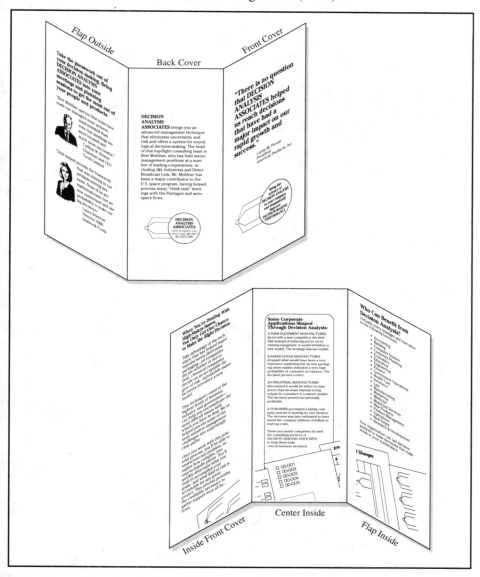

- The six-panel brochure on 8 1/2" x 11" paper or card stock is typically folded into thirds. The top illustration, above, shows the outside "spread" of three panels (including the front and back "covers"). The bottom illustration shows the inside "spread" of three panels. See the following two pages for larger views of the inside and outside panels.

"There is no question that DECISION ANALYSIS ASSOCIATES helped us reach decisions that have had a major impact on our rapid growth and success."

Curtis M. Proust
President
American Products, Inc.

Bring the science of DECISION ANALYSIS to your company and dramatically improve DECISION-MAKING PERFORMANCE

DECISION ANALYSIS ASSOCIATES brings you an advanced management technique that eliminates uncertainty and risk and offers a system for sound, logical decision-making. The head of this top-flight consulting team is Bret Mohlner, who has held senior management positions at a number of leading corporations, including J&L Industries and Direct Broadcast Link. Mr. Mohlner has been a major contributor to the U.S. space program, having helped process many "think tank" meetings with the Pentagon and aerospace firms.

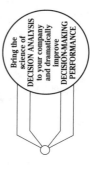

DECISION ANALYSIS ASSOCIATES
12210 Acropolis Court
Chevy Chase, MD 20815
301-555-7300

Take the guesswork out of your decision making. Bring DECISION ANALYSIS ASSOCIATES into your meetings and planning sessions to get the most out of your people and products.

"Bret Mohlner and his DAA team have made our managers more achievement-oriented than ever. Our meetings are more focused and much more successful."
Carlton W. Brister
Chairman and CEO
Tivoli Limited

"DAA helped provide the framework that was missing in our problem-solving sessions. None of us are mathematicians, but we now understand and use probability to make our big decisions."
Laura Seymour
Director, R&D
Seabrook Foods

Who Can Benefit from Decision Analysis?

Virtually every manager and executive in the following functions:

- Accounting
- Banking
- Computer Science
- Corporate Planning
- Economics
- Education
- Engineering
- Finance
- Government Operations
- Health Care
- Insurance
- Law
- Manufacturing
- Marketing
- Medicine
- Municipal Services
- New Products
- Product Management
- Operations
- Real Estate
- Research & Development

Your organization can use decision analysis to make decisions that make sense in your marketplace.

Effect of Changes

☐ 00-001
☐ 00-002
☐ 00-003
☐ 00-004
☐ 00-005

Some Corporate Applications Shaped Through Decision Analysis:

A FARM EQUIPMENT MANUFACTURER, faced with a new competitor, decided that instead of reducing prices on its existing equipment, it would introduce a new model. The strategy was successful.

A BAKED GOODS MANUFACTURER dropped what would have been a very expensive marketing test on new packaging when studies indicated a very high probability of consumer acceptance. The decision proved correct.

AN INDUSTRIAL MANUFACTURER determined it would be better to raise prices than increase manufacturing output for a product in a mature market. The decision proved exceptionally profitable.

A PUBLISHER purchased a failing company instead of starting its own division. The decision was later estimated to have saved the company millions of dollars in start-up costs.

These successful companies all used the consulting services of DECISION ANALYSIS ASSOCIATES to help them make critical business decisions

When You're Dealing With High-Stakes Issues, You Only Get One Chance to Make the Right Decision

Take advantage of the technique that has helped major manufacturers determine packaging...oil companies decide whether or not to drill...chemical companies decide on an acceptable degree of risk...automobile manufacturers introduce a new model.

This technique—used at the highest levels of business, industry, and government—can help you uncomplicate the most difficult issues with which you have to deal. We've helped process some of the most sensitive management challenges into surprisingly clear paths.

Once you work with this powerful process, you'll be able to restructure any problem, no matter how complex, into easy-to-handle pieces. You'll quickly determine what you need to accomplish your goals...and what kind of risk is acceptable for any given project. This process provides the credibility necessary to gather support from all factions.

- Testimonials bring credibility to a promotion.

- Listing types of organizations that can benefit from your services eliminates readers having to guess whether their company can benefit.

The focus of the brochure (4-29) shown at the right is on the consultant himself, from the photo on the front to the signature on the back. It gives the reader a sense of "knowing" the consultant even before a first meeting.

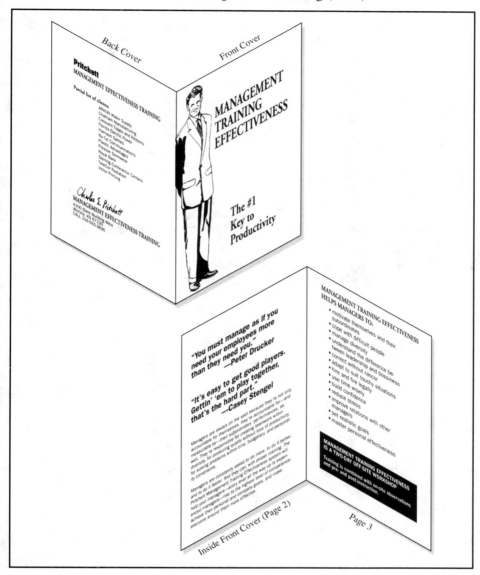

- The four-panel brochure on 8 1/2" x 11" paper or card stock is typically folded in half. The top illustration, above, shows the outside panels (the front and back "covers"). The bottom illustration shows the two inside panels. See the following two pages for larger views of the inside and outside panels.

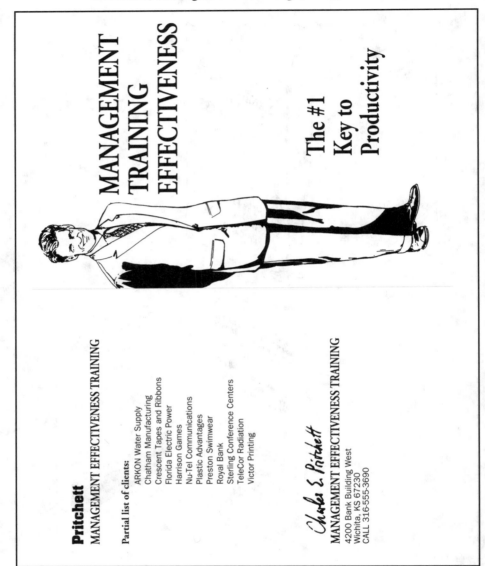

MANAGEMENT TRAINING EFFECTIVENESS

The #1 Key to Productivity

Pritchett
MANAGEMENT EFFECTIVENESS TRAINING

Partial list of clients:

ARKON Water Supply
Chatham Manufacturing
Crescent Tapes and Ribbons
Florida Electric Power
Harrison Games
Nu-Tel Communications
Plastic Advantages
Preston Swimwear
Royal Bank
Sterling Conference Centers
TeleCor Radiation
Victor Printing

Charles S. Pritchett
MANAGEMENT EFFECTIVENESS TRAINING

4200 Bank Building West
Wichita, KS 67230
CALL 316-555-3690

MANAGEMENT TRAINING EFFECTIVENESS HELPS MANAGERS TO:

- motivate themselves and their subordinates
- cope with difficult people
- manage diversity
- understand the difference between leadership and bossiness
- correct without rancor
- adapt to suit touchy situations
- hire and fire legally
- use time wisely
- build confidence
- reduce stress
- improve relations with other managers
- set realistic goals
- master personal effectiveness

MANAGEMENT TRAINING EFFECTIVENESS IS A TWO-DAY OFF-SITE WORKSHOP

Training is combined with on-site observations and pre- and post-instruction.

"You must manage as if you need your employees more than they need you."
—Peter Drucker

"It's easy to get good players. Gettin' 'em to play together, that's the hard part."
—Casey Stengel

Managers are always on the spot because they're not only accountable for themselves, they're accountable for—and measurable by—their subordinates' performances, as well. They're responsible for creating teamwork within diversity, for producing quality without loss of productivity, for solving problems within time, budgetary, and personality constraints.

Managers are constantly asked to do more, to do it better, and to do it faster. And they can, with proper training. The Pritchett Management Training Effectiveness system will help your managers—entry level all the way up to experienced managers—rise to the highest level of competence, achieve their personal and company goals, and make everyone around them more effective.

- Presenting benefits helps the reader visualize the service.

- Listing clients offers prospects a sense of security about your firm.

A humorous illustration like the one on the front of the brochure (4-30) shown at the right will quickly grab the attention of the reader. But be sure it relates directly to your services, and that it is in good taste.

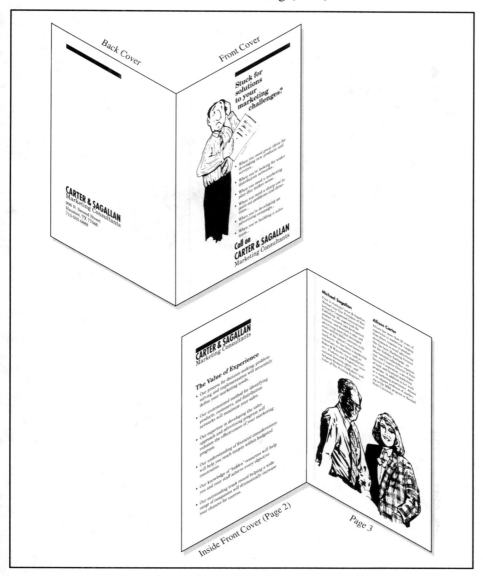

• The four-panel brochure on 8 1/2" x 11" paper or card stock is typically folded in half. The top illustration, above, shows the outside panels (the front and back "covers"). The bottom illustration shows the two inside panels. See the following two pages for larger views of the inside and outside panels.

CARTER & SAGALLAN
Marketing Consultants

The Value of Experience

- Our process for decision-making, problem-solving and implementation will accurately define your marketing needs.

- Our systematized method for identifying products, customers, and distribution networks will maximize your sales.

- Our expertise in developing the sales approach and advertising program will enhance the effectiveness of your marketing program.

- Our understanding of financial considerations will help you reach targets within budgeted constraints.

- Our knowledge of "hidden" resources will help you and your staff achieve every objective.

- Our outstanding track record helping a wide range of companies will dramatically increase your chances for success.

Michael Sagallan

Prior to starting Carter & Sagallan, Michael was Vice President of Marketing for Longwood International Publishing. He supervised the product research and development function, and directed a sales and advertising team that developed multi-million dollar contracts with many of the nation's best-known marketers. He has been a marketing consultant to companies such as Baker & Waverly (toy manufacturers), Products and Properties (international licensing agent), and Seligson Brothers Publishers (publisher of The Printing Register).

Allison Carter

Allison has more than 20 years of experience in marketing, ranging from direct response to product development to retail advertising. She has been Marketing Director for the Halliday Exchange, an international collectibles organization, and Creative Director of Data Services Corporation, a developer of bank and financial marketing programs. In addition to her work as a marketing practitioner, Allison is an adjunct professor at Kendall State University.

- The more you spell out your areas of expertise, the more you increase the chance of an inquiry.

- Prospects want to know who they're dealing with. Background information about the principals, including clients served, is a good way to assure them.

Company
Address
City, State Zip

Put the most advanced computer system
specifically designed
for the service and repair industry
to work for you...FREE!

Dear Accounting Manager:

You may be eligible to participate in ACS' FREE one-day demonstration program to see for yourself how you can save time and money through updated technology. If you are currently using an accounting software package, one of our experienced consultants will spend a full day with you—or someone you designate.

1. In the morning, your ACS consultant will sit with you and your staff as you go about your normal procedures.
2. During mid-day, your ACS consultant will set up a prototype system using a laptop computer.
3. In the afternoon, your ACS consultant will process work orders and invoices, schedule planned maintenance visits, and process any other transactions you want to see, using real data you supply.
4. Within one week, your ACS consultant will issue a Systems Analysis Report detailing the strengths and weaknesses of your current system. There is no charge for any of these procedures.

That's how confident we are that we can help you save time and money. We'd like the opportunity to show you how much you have to gain by upgrading your system.

Call me at 805-555-4422 for details. Or return the card in the enclosed brochure and we'll follow up.

Sincerely,

Lynne Jefferson

- By confining the special offer to just the letter, you give your brochure longer life.

- Be certain to headline your special offer. Don't make the reader search for it.

Company
Address
City, State Zip

It doesn't matter if you have
hundreds of dollars or thousands of dollars
to invest. What matters is that you make the
best possible investment decision for your needs.

Dear Investor:

In a world where borders are shrinking and investment opportunities are growing...where new tax laws and regulations impact your
investments before you know it...where risk and reward are
confused and misunderstood...you need, more than ever, to
understand which investments make the most sense for you, your
family, and your business.

We can help you sort through the changes and the choices that
confront every investor today—large and small. We can help you
analyze investments that make sense for today and for tomorrow.
We can help you as we've helped hundreds of others put their
assets to work and take advantage of the exciting diversity
available to today's investor.

Call us for an appointment (804-555-6633). Meet with financial
planners who have guided hundreds to secure and satisfying
investments. Become a part of the Roberts & Roberts family.

Sincerely,

Melvyn and Edwin Roberts

- Describe your prospect's concerns in such a way that they can understand the value of
  your services.

- It's not necessary to personalize a mass mailing such as this one. A generic salutation,
  such as "Dear Investor," does the job.

Company
Address
City, State Zip

Date

Mr. George Greene
U.S. Naval Command
Whittier Supply Center
13 Howard Commons
Whittier, CA 90610

Dear Mr. Greene:

Many of the problems you face defy intuitive solutions...and are full of uncertainty and risk. But every situation—no matter how tentative or unsettling it seems—can be logically analyzed and systematically mapped out.

With Decision Analysis Associates' techniques you'll have a basis for cutting through complex issues. You'll have a quantitative system that will win converts to your position and strengthen your organization's leadership role. Decision Analysis Associates will improve your decision-making process immediately.

We've had the opportunity to work with groups at Fort McNair, Fort Ord, and the Pentagon. I'm confident we can duplicate the success we've had with other military organizations.

After you've had a chance to review this material, I'll call to arrange for an appointment. I appreciate your interest.

Sincerely,

Bret Mohlner

- Offer examples of consulting jobs that are in similar fields.

- Don't forget that a cover letter is a sales letter. It should be able to stand alone from the brochure, even though it complements it.

Company
Address
City, State Zip

Date

Mr. Charles Martin
InterState Banking Corp.
2 InterState Drive
North Wales, PA 19454

Dear Mr. Martin:

Would the managers of your bank say the following are true about them?

1. At least 3/4 of my day is planned before I start work.
2. I'm aware of key company events over the next 2-4 weeks.
3. I plan for free time to handle unanticipated events.
4. People come to me for ideas on how they can improve.
5. I continually update my plans and files so someone could fill in for me in the event of a long absence.
6. I evaluate time-wasting activities that hinder my performance.
7. My supervisor considers me to be an effective manager.

May I offer you a complete copy of my management test? It will help you determine where your managers are weakest...and what skills need upgrading. The enclosed brochure highlights significant growth that employees have experienced through my management training program.

I'll call for an appointment.

Sincerely,

Charles Prichett

- Involvement devices (e.g., questions) ensure readership.

- Offering something of value to the reader helps get an appointment.

Company
Address
City, State Zip

Date

Ms. Joanne Zelman
Starburst Business Forms
56 Industrial Highway
Dayton, OH 45470

Dear Ms. Zelman:

I appreciate the time you gave me on the phone. And I'm sure that once we have the opportunity to work together, you'll agree it was time well spent.

The enclosed brochure details our complete services, but since you're trying to determine how to bolster your sales force, you may be particularly interested in our credentials in that area.

My partner, Michael Sagallan has hired, trained, and managed a number of very successful sales forces. Michael and I both have extensive experience in the development and use of sales support materials, mailings and advertisements. And I have a particularly strong background in data support and evaluative systems.

We're knowledgeable, resourceful sales and marketing professionals. And we'd like the opportunity to discuss our services and how they might mesh with your needs. I'll call next week to arrange a meeting.

Cordially,

Allison Carter

- The more you can customize your cover letter to meet your prospects' needs and expectations, the greater the likelihood of getting appointments and contracts.

- Always indicate that an action (e.g., a phone call, proposal, visit) will follow. Don't just hope that the recipient will follow up on their own.

Cut
Telecommunications
Spending

Halt spiraling telecommunications costs. Let a telecommunications "insider" review
and evaluate your systems and
expenses. FREE APPRAISAL
from DataCom Associates.
Call 1-800-555-1717 for information.

- Make your advertising dollars pay off by selecting publications that target your specific audiences (e.g., MIS managers, controllers)

- Don't try to tell an entire story in small classified space. Focus on a key benefit or issue.

Raise the Capital That Will:

- **Launch Your New Venture**
- **Finance Your New Product**
- **Support Your New Service**

It's easy to get the capital you need...if you know how! Our consulting team will help you avoid the pitfalls and match you with the right venture capital group.

Receive free information with absolutely no cost or obligation

FINANCIAL SERVICES GROUP, INC.
9202 Biltmore Road/Suite 1900
Waco, TX 76701

Call today and kick-start your future
1-817-555-0304

- Quickly explain the benefits of your service.

- The words "no cost or obligation" are reassuring to many people who are afraid of high pressure sales pitches.

Return the coupon below and receive a FREE COPY of the WORK AND FAMILY ISSUES SURVEY detailing how innovative companies resolve family problems that impact on absenteeism and productivity.

Mail to: W.K. Black & Associates, Dept. 21
113 Fellowship Road, Camden, New Jersey 08110

OR CALL 1-609-555-1822

☐ YES! Send me a FREE COPY of the
WORK AND FAMILY ISSUES SURVEY.

Name _____

Title _____

Company _____

Address _____

City _____ State _____ Zip _____

Phone _____ Ext. _____

- An advertisement that offers something of perceived value will draw top response. Surveys are attention-getters.

- Make your coupon large enough to be usable.

Design & **T**echnology **C**onsultants

State of the art computer aided design capability:

- ▲▲ Solid modeling
- ▲▲ Finite element modeling
- ▲▲ Structural analysis
- ▲▲ Frame analysis
- ▲▲ Beam analysis
- ▲▲ System dynamics
- ▲▲ Model solution
- ▲▲ Test data analysis
- ▲▲ Complete documentation

High-tech solutions for all your design and engineering requirements.

CARL SPENCER & ASSOCIATES, INC.
20 Gibbstown-Blenheim Road
Linkwood, MD 21835

301-555-9009

- An ad in a trade magazine targeted to the readers' industry can reap rewards. Advertising in several consecutive issues is the key to building awareness of your company.

- Take enough space to highlight all your capabilities.

Wechter International, Inc.
Information & Telecommunication
Systems Consulting
Strategic Systems Planning
Training

FREE BROCHURE
Call 800-555-1314
1220 Berwyn Road/Wayne, PA 19087

- People equate display ads with bigger and better companies. Consider upgrading from a simple listing.

- Detailing your specialties will avoid unnecessary calls and wasted time.

NARR: If you've lost your job or want to move into a better one, listen to what Tom Stampley has to say about Scott Herman Associates:

MAN: I can't believe what Scott Herman Associates did for me. After the devastation of an unexpected layoff, they had me in the marketplace in a matter of days.

NARR: And here's how Sara Fargo described our employment counseling service:

WOMAN: Just when I thought I was going to have to move, Scott Herman Associates helped me identify employers right around the corner! For the first time in my life, I have a commute of less than 10 minutes. I'm right where I want to be, thanks to you.

NARR: And John Stearns may have summed us up best when he said:

MAN: Scott Herman Associates built up my self-confidence. They worked with me until I got just the job I wanted.

NARR: Not a week goes by without similar comments. We prepare people to identify and step into rewarding, challenging jobs. We put your life and your career into focus and help you explore the marketplace as you've never done before.

You've worked hard to get where you are. Now let us show you how to get the job you really want... and really deserve.

Scott Herman Associates will get you where you want to go. We've been doing it for Bay area residents since 1974. Call one of our employment consultants at 415-555-JOBS. That's 415-555-JOBS for the happiness, contentment, and fulfillment that the right career offers.

- Radio advertising can be efficient if you have the kind of service that attracts a wide base. It's good, for example, for an employment consultant, but not nearly as effective for an engineering consulting firm.

- The script should be written so it can be pared down into a number of versions. For example, this script can easily be shortened by cutting some of the testimonials.

NETWORKING CHECKLIST

_____ **PROFESSIONAL DIRECTORIES**
Use the membership directories of any organizations
to which you belong. Professional contacts are
excellent networking sources.

_____ **BUSINESS ASSOCIATES**
Contact people you've met in your career. They represent
potential assignments or referrals.

_____ **CURRENT AND PAST CLIENTS**
Contact people with whom you've done business. They are
an excellent source for referrals.

_____ **FRIENDS, NEIGHBORS AND RELATIVES**
Contact anyone who might possibly be in a position to help
you. But don't expect them to read your mind; ask for
help and you'll get it.

_____ **NONCOMPETING CONSULTANTS**
Contact people you've met at professional meetings, or
whom you can consider calling or writing even if you
don't know them. Offer them an arrangement where
they'll provide references to your service and you'll
do the same for them.

_____ **FORMER EMPLOYERS**
Contact people you've worked for. Previous employers are
excellent sources for immediate consulting jobs and
referrals. And if they're willing to give you referrals, they're
also willing to recommend you.

• This is not the time for shyness; call upon any and all resources.

• Be sure to thank anyone whose networking suggestions were helpful.

Company Name
Address
City, State Zip

Date

Mr. John J. Morgan
Senior Vice President
Larini & Mitchell Concrete Co.
1313 Bayview Road
Richmond, VA 23234

Dear John:

Recently, I thought about the work I did last month with your Safety Committee. As we both know, it was an important project that neither of us had anticipated or even scheduled as a priority. It occurred to me that if a progressive company like yours had benefitted from the project, other companies might also want to consider the kind of program I developed for you.

As you know, I have had some preliminary conversations with Frank Markham at Andrews Pharmaceuticals. We are stuck in a pre-proposal stage until he makes some budget decisions for next year. Would it be presumptuous of me to ask for your help?

I'd be very appreciative if you would call or write Frank to describe the tremendous cost benefits you received from our project. You know how important I believe our recent work was, both from an environmental perspective and in terms of personal safety for the people at your plant.

I thank you for any help you can give me. I am heading to Atlanta tonight, but I will call you early next week when I return.

Kindest regards,

Martin Schine

- Your best source of new business will probably come from referrals from satisfied clients. Don't be shy about asking them, but do it in a way that will not make them feel pressured.

- It's helpful if the client understands why you are asking for the referral, not only so that they can gear their comments to your needs, but also so that they can feel part of the process.

Letter Thanking Client For Referral (4-44)

Company Name
Address
City, State Zip

Date

Mr. John J. Morgan
Senior Vice President
Larini & Mitchell Concrete Co.
1313 Bayview Road
Richmond, VA 23234

Dear John:

Thank you for your very complimentary letter to Frank Markham at
Andrews Pharmaceuticals. Your kind words certainly expedited
our discussions and got me in front of his committee for a formal
presentation last week.

There are a number of other priorities that Andrews needs to
address before the project gets support from their senior management team. Frank has been optimistic and supportive in our
conversations. He has also encouraged me to be patient with
their decision-making process. I am confident that I will get the
call when they decide to move forward. I have you to thank for
that!

I hope you know just how much I appreciate your friendship and
your professional support. Thanks again for taking the time to
write to Frank. If all goes well, I should be in your area next
month. I'll call to see if you are free for lunch.

Kindest regards,

Martin Schine

• Be sure to thank a client for a referral, even if it doesn't get you the desired results.

• As a courtesy, inform your client of the status of the project. And follow up at the
conclusion of the process with the ultimate outcome.

Marketing— 5
Indirect Methods

Indirect methods of marketing should be an important part of your overall growth plan. They are more long term than the direct methods that were highlighted in Chapter 4. Indirect methods have a cumulative effect: They build name recognition and credibility over a period of time. The techniques include:

- Public speaking
- Seminars
- Professional affiliations
- Writing books and articles
- Public relations
- Newsletters

Public Speaking

Depending on your consulting specialty, there may be enormous benefits in speaking before groups. Audience members may be able to use your services or recommend you to friends or business associates. Speaking before fraternal, civic, business, government, or industry groups will earn you valuable exposure, credibility and, ultimately, new clients. So why do so many consultants avoid doing it?

One answer seems to be obvious—fear, commonly referred to as "stage fright." Another answer is a lack of understanding of what needs to be done to be a good public speaker. Not surprisingly, fear can be overcome by learning the essentials of successful public speaking. In fact, if you are willing to take the time to master the steps that follow, you need never again be traumatized by the prospect of public speaking. Also refer to the Public Speaking Checklist (5-01), at the end of the chapter.

1. **Preparation: Know Your Audience.** The biggest error in public speaking is not paying enough attention to who will be receiving

your message. By learning about the audience beforehand, you'll know how well acquainted they are with the subject of your speech—and, therefore, how best to present your material.

2. **Organization: Make It Easy to Follow.** Your speech must have a defined structure: an identifiable beginning, middle and end. You should deal with one major point, usually in the form of an opportunity or a problem. At the beginning of the speech, present your key point clearly and simply, after first getting the attention of the audience.

   During the middle of the speech, focus on how the audience can benefit from the opportunity or solve the problem you have presented. Support your points with facts, enthusiasm, and positive outcomes.

   At the end of the speech, restate the key point so the audience will be crystal-clear as to what you want them to remember, and what action, if any, you want them to take. The speechmaker's credo is (a) tell them what you're going to say, (b) say it, and (c) tell them what you said.

3. **Presentation: Select the Format that Fits.** To be comfortable in front of a group, it's important to have materials in a format that provides the highest level of confidence. For example, if you're new to public speaking, you may want to have a complete script in front of you for your presentation. Although experienced speakers rarely use a fully-scripted speech, it may be a good idea for novices because it eliminates the stress of trying to memorize. Unfortunately, reading can sound monotonous, and can prevent the speaker from maintaining eye contact—both significant ways to lose the audience's attention. So if you must read, vary your tone and speed, and look up from your script as frequently as possible.

   Experienced speakers prefer outlines or notes. No matter how well they know their subject matter, good speakers don't risk losing a major point. They rely on notes to keep them on track. Large note cards are recommended, and they should be numbered in case they are dropped or somehow get out of order. The only thing worse than no notes are out-of-order notes. Note cards should always be marked to coincide with any visuals ("Flip switch," "Change to Overhead #4," "Show poster.").

4. **Equipment: Don't Leave It to Chance.** Audiovisual aids are excellent in helping the audience focus on a specific topic or concept, and reinforcing what you're discussing. They engage the

audience, raising their retention level. The audience can literally see what you're saying. Visual aids are helpful in presenting facts and figures, and in simplifying complex processes and ideas. And they can dramatize your message. Visual aids that can be of value in public speaking and seminars include:

- Slides
- Flipcharts (for smaller groups only)
- Blackboard/Whiteboard (for smaller groups only)
- Overhead transparencies
- Videotapes and films
- Handouts

If you're using audiovisual equipment, get in the habit of (a) arriving early to familiarize yourself with the equipment, and (b) planning what you'll do if the equipment fails. Experienced speakers prepare for the unexpected.

5. **Self-Evaluation: Practice, Practice, Practice.** Observing yourself in the act of giving a speech will improve your public speaking dramatically. The ideal way to practice is in front of a videotape camera. If you don't have one available, present your speech to a friend for their comments. At the least, make an audiotape of your presentation and listen to it to understand how others will hear you.

Strive for naturalness and a body language that matches the style of your speech. And *don't* be too surprised by what you see and hear during your practice sessions. *Do* be concerned about how you stand and use your arms, and what your delivery sounds like.

Finally, listen to the reactions and the constructive criticism of your audience during the actual presentation. Solicit feedback on your speech. Hand out an evaluation form that allows for anonymous critiquing. Refer to the Speaker Evaluation Form (5-02) found later in the chapter.

Organization-Sponsored Seminars

If you've ever attended a seminar (which can range from a half-day to one, two, or more days), you're aware of the presumption by the audience that the seminar leader is someone at the top of their field.

That's just one reason that many consultants jump at the opportunity to conduct a free seminar—they're assured of having an audience of potential clients. If you specialize, for example, in plant and office layout consulting, and a trade association offers you the opportunity to conduct a seminar on work flow dynamics for 30 facilities managers, would you take the job in the hope of generating future business from the attendees?

You probably should! Think about how much it would cost you to contact and visit 30 prospects at their offices. With estimates of the cost of a sales call running upwards of $700 per visit, it would cost you $21,000 to see each of the participants separately. And there's the added benefit of having the prospects view you as a respected, in-demand expert, not as a salesperson.

There are a number of other good reasons why you should consider presenting seminars to organizations:

- **Little expense**—It usually doesn't cost a penny (other than your time) to conduct a seminar for an organization, professional society or industry association. You don't have to lay out money for administrative details (registrations, collections, questions, facilities arrangements), mail and phone solicitations, and food service. The organization does it all for you, including transportation, food and lodging if required.

- **Wide exposure**—Publicity has a cumulative effect. When you agree to conduct a seminar for an organization, your name appears many times in all kinds of literature. Suppose, for example, you're asked to present a seminar for a local chapter of a national nonprofit organization. The local chapter will include mention of your name and specialty in its newsletter. There may be a meeting announcement mailed to members as well as to other lists, putting your name in front of hundreds of more people.

  The national organization may pick up a news item about the seminar, as might local media (radio and television often promote nonprofit organizations). But you might not want to depend on the organization's ability to contact the media. Later in this chapter, you'll learn about some of the techniques for generating publicity for yourself. Keep in mind that everything you do is newsworthy. It's your responsibility to be certain that everyone is aware of your professional activities.

  One consultant tells of the time an advertisement for one of his seminars was mentioned in a local newspaper. A visiting businessperson saw the notice but *didn't* attend the seminar. However, because of the subject matter, he contacted the consultant afterwards, and they eventually concluded a $150,000 consulting contract.

- **Useful feedback**—Use your seminars to listen to what the audience is saying. Listening is a skill that six-figure salespeople use with great success, and it's a skill that you must master to be a successful consultant. Learn what your market wants and use that information to generate new consulting business.

Creating Your Own Seminars

You can also create your own seminar and:

1. Promote it to industry groups (or the general public, depending on your specialty), possibly to generate a profit from the seminar itself by charging a fee. More likely, however, you'll use the seminar to demonstrate your expertise, so that you can convert attendees into future consulting clients.
2. Create customized versions that can be conducted "in-house" for client organizations for a fee.
3. Videotape your seminar and lend the tape to organizations to promote your services. Also, depending on the subject of your presentation, you may be able to sell videotapes to those interested in the information presented.

The Seminar Checklist (5-03) contains items that will help you present a successful seminar, whether for organizations or on your own. It is found at the end of the chapter.

Marketing Your Seminar

Direct mail (see Chapter 4) tends to be the most effective vehicle for reaching large numbers of potential attendees. Assuming that your seminar is business-related, there are many business lists available for your use. If your seminar appeals to a specific job title, such as Chief Financial Officer, you can easily target that group.

On the other hand, if your market is more diverse (for example, individuals who might be interested in an investment or retirement seminar), you'll probably want to advertise in local newspapers. Tailor your advertising medium to your particular audience.

Two ads for marketing seminars (5-04 and 5-05) are found later in the chapter.

Joining Professional Associations

According to one consultant, joining professional organizations was an important step in building his business. In his case, the consultant joined a local chapter of the American Society for Training & Development (ASTD), a Washington, D.C. group comprised of 40,000 human resource development professionals.

The original motivation to join was economic. The consultant was told by another consultant (networking in action!) that most ASTD members were potential clients. As the consultant began to attend meetings and got to know the other members, he became involved with the organization, eventually serving two terms as chapter president. It was the best of all worlds: The consultant generated business, and gave back to the group as much as he gained.

There were other benefits, as well. The consultant had the opportunity to meet other consultants, and they created their own informal network. Leads were swapped, strategies discussed, advice offered, and subcontracting work often resulted. And long-term friendships were formed.

By joining professional groups, you also have access to their membership directories, which usually provide names, addresses and phone numbers. Although every group has its own set of rules about how the names may be used, as a member you are always within your rights to contact other members.

Once you join a professional organization, it becomes a part of your "resume." Professional membership lends credibility to your company and your consulting services.

If you need help in finding appropriate associations, your local library should have a copy of *The Encyclopedia of Associations* (published by Gale Research) in its research section. This 3-volume set includes listings of virtually every membership group in the country.

Writing Articles

Some consultants view the practice of writing articles for magazines, journals and newspapers as income opportunities. Others see article writing as a public relations opportunity, and are unconcerned with the modest fees it can generate. Writing articles provides consultants with a chance to have their names and expertise displayed before thousands of readers, some of whom are prospective clients.

Many successful consultants point to articles they've written as having generated long-term clients. One consultant said that he still gets an occasional call about an article he wrote for a professional journal more than ten years ago. Because it was so well-received, he includes that article in the literature packet he gives to prospective clients.

It should go without saying that you need to match your expertise to the periodicals and their readers. If you're planning on writing a technical piece on cost reductions for satellite transmission, you should confine your submission to appropriate engineering journals. If you're writing an article on how technology breakthroughs are going to result in new forms of home entertainment, try to place it in newspapers and consumer-oriented magazines.

If you think you have something to say, you'll first want to be certain that an editor agrees it's worth publishing. Good writing is a difficult and time-consuming process, even for professionals. Before you spend the time, it makes sense to submit a proposal, particularly for feature length articles.

If you're looking for sources of magazines and journals that may be interested in publishing your articles, *Standard Rate and Data Service* reference books can be found in larger libraries. There's one for business journals, one for consumer magazines, and one for newspapers. Listings include names, addresses, and phone numbers, along with descriptions of the editorial focus of the publications.

There's an additional way to take advantage of your writing ability. Letters to the Editor are traditionally among the best read sections in newspapers and magazines. If you're at odds with an issue mentioned in an article, and you can supply a well thought out response, you'll have a good opportunity to be published. A reader who shares your point of view may be inclined to call you. Be sure to list yourself—in articles as well as letters to the editor—as a consultant. Remember, indirect marketing is cumulative. Get your name out as much as possible.

An Article Proposal Worksheet (5-06) is found later in the chapter.

Writing Books

Many consultants have the material for a publishable book or self-improvement program (e.g., audio or videocassette) within the work they have already created for clients.

One labor and employment relations consultant suddenly realized that the information he had developed over the years for his clients formed the basis of a book that could help benefit every personnel department in the country.

Sometimes it's difficult to see that you've amassed a body of knowledge that has far-ranging application. Step back and think about what you've created for your clients, and you might see that you have something to offer thousands of other companies with similar problems and challenges.

If you become the author of a published book, you'll have a distinct edge over competitors who have not been published. There's power and credibility in the printed word that transfers to increased requests for consulting work. The primary value of writing a business book is to display your expertise. It is not, contrary to most expectations, a method for becoming rich. With the exception of a relatively small handful of authors, the royalties earned from writing a business book rarely amount to much. But the prestige that accompanies author-ship of a book can help generate a lifetime of consulting assignments. That's what makes the painstaking process worth the time and effort.

There are three primary ways to publish. One is through traditional publishing firms, a second is through professional/special interest groups, and the third is to self-publish. Traditional or special interest publishing may be the first option for many consultants because, other than the writing, the publisher does everything (typesetting, design, distribution, marketing). On the other hand, self-publishing offers certain incentives: You can keep a far larger share of the selling price, in contrast to a 5%-10% author's royalty. And you don't have to compromise on content.

1. **Traditional publishers.** One way to determine the companies best suited to publish your book is to look for similar titles in your bookstore. Most publishers specialize in a particular market such as small businesses, professionals, etc. Choose the publishers that best fit the kind of book you have in mind.

   To confirm your selection—and get information about whom to contact and their address— head to the reference section of your library and look at *Literary Market Place* (LMP). This directory lists virtually every publisher in the United States and Canada, and includes contact names, addresses, phone numbers, and, importantly, the specialties of each publisher. LMP also lists hundreds of book publishing consultants, colleagues who may be able to offer services in editing, advertising, promotion, produc-tion, finance, management, marketing and printing. The names may be of particular value if you decide to self-publish.

2. **Special interest publishers.** Most large professional societies and universities have publishing arms and are listed in *Literary Market Place*. If you don't know which associations might be interested, begin your search with *The Encyclopedia of Associa-tions* to determine the names of the organizations involved in your specialty, then check LMP to confirm that they publish in your area of expertise, or to obtain a contact name. Special interest publishers aren't looking for bestsellers; they're often more interested in publications that have value to members.

3. **Self-publishing.** Many consultants, particularly those who speak publicly or conduct seminars, offer published products for sale at "the back of the room" at the conclusion of the seminar. Some consultants consider the sale of their own published materials a very important part of their practice.

Self-published materials can take the form of a tape or transcript of a seminar or workshop, a looseleaf book with strategies for implementing whatever the topic of the program is, inexpensive stapled reports, or books or tapes. Some speakers purchase other consultants' tapes and books (at a discount) and offer them as part of the mix.

If you believe you have something to say and you're determined to self-publish, you might be surprised at how inexpensive it can be. If you're equipped for desktop publishing (and possess a good laser-quality printer) you can produce the typeset pages necessary to print. Even if you can't, simply give your disk to a typesetter, and have the pages produced at a fraction of the cost of regular typesetting.

Although it's rare for a self-published book to go into general distribution, it has happened. If you feel you have a book (or audio or video tape) with wide appeal, contact one of any number of book wholesalers you'll find listed in *Literary Market Place*. Or, using the same publication, look for a publisher that also distributes other books in addition to their own. Your other option is to sell your publications via mail order.

Many consultants reap publicity from one or more of the three forms of publishing. A press release about your publishing venture, such as one of those found at the end of the chapter, will usually be picked up by various media, and may possibly earn you favorable reviews, as well as numerous leads.

A Book Proposal Worksheet (5-07) is also located at the end of the chapter.

Public Relations

The United States was built on public relations. Our revered revolutionary patriots were masters of public relations who knew how to use their words to convert the public to their point of view. Not much has changed in the 200 or so years since. Public relations is still a powerful marketing tool.

Every speaking engagement, every seminar, every article, book or tape you produce provides you with an opportunity to present your practice to prospects and clients in a highly credible way—by generating free publicity through press releases.

If you have something newsworthy that would be of interest to a magazine's or newspaper's readers, or radio and television viewers, the chances are pretty good that your information will be published.

The news media need to disseminate news. Without a steady flow, presses would stop and broadcast stations would have "dead air." It's the news media's job to find material of interest to readers, and it's your job to convince them that you have what they're looking for. Follow these guidelines to ensure the greatest chance for success.

- **Present your press releases the way editors want them prepared**. They must be dated (to show that they're current), and they must state when the information may be released. In most cases, writers will indicate "For Immediate Release," telling the editors it's okay to use the story right away. There should also be a contact name and phone number listed. Nothing will kill a story faster than an editor who is unable to find someone knowledgeable to speak with about a press release.

  Double space your copy (this gives editors room to edit), and use only one side of a sheet of paper. If the release runs more than one page, indicate the number of pages on the first page, much as you would on a fax (e.g., Page 1 of 3), and be sure to number the succeeding pages (Page 2 of 3, etc.).

  Use the article-ending symbols recognized by all editors: "30" or "###." Whichever symbol you select should be centered under the last line of copy in your story. This also tells an editor that the release was sent by someone who knows their business.

  Use a "newsy" headline, not a "cutesy" one. "Albert Moore Named Man of the Year" may not start one's blood racing, but it will draw a glance from a local editor. Something like "And the Winner is..." is apt to be deposited in the circular file. The less an editor has to rewrite a press release, the better the chance it will be published.

- **Match your stories to your media.** While an engineering journal might be excited about running a story on "finite element modeling/analysis of composites, including EIRP and GT contour analysis," your local newspaper's business section will not. The same story might be submitted to the town newspaper as "Local Consultant Wins Key Government Contract."

  A focus on local news is what distinguishes daily and weekly newspapers from larger regional and national papers. Even though the dailies and weeklies run many of the same stories as their larger counterparts, it is the local "angle" that brings them readership. Tailor your release to be of interest to a local audience, and you'll generate publicity for your consultancy.

  Radio and television are much more difficult to break into, due to limitations of air time. To get on television news, you have to have a visual slant to your release. A conference or trade show has a better chance of gaining coverage than an announcement about a promotion or a new client. A health breakthrough may gain television time, but moving your office will not. You have an excellent chance of receiving television and radio time (at least as a public service announcement) if you are conducting a seminar or making a speech for a nonprofit organization.

- **Use simple English.** If you want to get your press releases published in general interest publications, put your industry jargon aside. If an editor has to use a dictionary to understand the release, you're in trouble. Use short sentences and short paragraphs.

    Every journalist (whether writing for print or broadcast media) is trained to answer five key questions: Who, what, where, when, and why. When you write a press release, be sure you, too, answer all those questions within the first paragraph or two.

- **Don't waste an editor's time and your money.** Submit each press release to the proper person. It's tempting to mail a release to hundreds of editors representing many different kinds of readers. But all you'll do, in addition to wasting paper and postage, is alienate editors by sending them material they can't possibly use.

    If your press releases are going to a wide audience, you can put together your publicity lists through the *Standard Rate & Data Service* directories for business magazines, consumer magazines, newspapers, radio and television, or through publications such as *Beacon's Publicity Checker*, both of which are available at larger libraries.

A series of press releases (5-08 through 5-17) is found at the end of the chapter.

Newsletters

Newsletters provide an excellent means of impressing prospects with your knowledge and professionalism. They also provide an effective way to maintain relationships with clients. Bi-monthly, quarterly, or even semi-annual newsletters containing information relevant to readers keep you and your image as a professional in front of your primary markets.

Your most current newsletter should be included with any promotional mailings you make to prospects. And editors of business columns at your local newspaper, industry publications and regional business magazines should be on your newsletter mailing list.

In addition to news, views and advice about your area of specialization, include announcements about your upcoming speeches and seminars as well as recaps after the speeches and seminars have been delivered. Feature any industry research you may have conducted, and hints and tips that will be of value to your readers.

Consider hiring a professional writer to prepare the copy for the newsletter, even though you will be giving the writer the information to use. The time and talent it takes to write a good newsletter is best left to a professional. Think seriously of hiring a designer to create the newsletter's format. After the first edition, you can turn the production over to a local desktop publishing company and instruct them to stay with the format you've already paid for.

A Newsletter (5-18) is found at the end of the chapter.

PUBLIC SPEAKING CHECKLIST

1. AUDIENCE
A. What is audience's level of knowledge of your topic?

_____
_____
_____
_____
_____
_____

B. What kind of impact can they have on your business?

_____
_____
_____
_____
_____
_____

C. What do you hope will result from your speech?

_____
_____
_____
_____
_____
_____

2. ORGANIZATION
A. Problem or opportunity to be presented

_____
_____
_____
_____
_____
_____

B. Solution or benefit offered

_____
_____
_____
_____
_____
_____

C. Supporting information or data

_____
_____
_____
_____
_____
_____

D. Restate points A, B, C

3. PRESENTATION METHODS
   A. Fully scripted. Not recommended by professionals. Tendency to read, producing monotone, losing eye contact. Recommended only for nervous novices.
   B. Outline. Allows speaker to appear extemporaneous; provides opportunity to ad lib without losing track.
   C. Note cards. Use 3x5 or 4x6 cards. Number them (if dropped, you can quickly find your place).
   D. Extemporaneous. Even best speakers use a "prompt." You're flirting with danger not to have notes of some sort.
   E. Audiovisual equipment. Make notes to indicate when to flip to the next visual. Practice so you don't have to look for the switch. Check equipment before any speech. Have a back-up plan in case of mechanical failure.

- Henry Ford said that "Getting ready is the secret of success." By reviewing this checklist before a speech, you will always prepare for success.

- Audiences expect you to be good. Present yourself professionally, and you won't disappoint them.

Speaker Evaluation Form (5-02)

SPEAKER EVALUATION FORM

Name of Speaker: _____

Topic: _____

(Circle One)
Excellent — Poor

1. Did the speaker have command of
   the material?   5 4 3 2 1

2. Did the speaker maintain your
   interest throughout?   5 4 3 2 1

3. Did the speaker answer questions
   to your satisfaction?   5 4 3 2 1

4. Did the speaker deal with the topic
   you expected?   5 4 3 2 1

5. Were you able to see overheads,
   slides, etc.?   5 4 3 2 1

6. Were the handouts of value?   5 4 3 2 1

7. Do you have a better understanding
   of this topic because of the talk?   5 4 3 2 1

8. Overall, how would you rate the presentation?   5 4 3 2 1

Comments:

_____
_____
_____
_____
_____

- Don't be afraid to solicit comments. You'll (a) learn from the criticism, and (b) use the comments to prepare for your next speech.

- Be sure that this form looks as good as the rest of your presentation. A badly photocopied or printed form makes you look unprofessional.

SEMINAR CHECKLIST

SPONSORSHIP
Will the seminar be sponsored? _____

If so, by what organization?

_____

Will the sponsoring organization generate publicity? _____

PUBLICITY
Do I need to do my own publicity? _____

If so, who should receive publicity? _____

_____

What media should I use to promote the seminar?
_____
_____

AUDIENCE
Who is the audience? _____

_____

Does the subject matter and level of the seminar match the audience?

_____

THE SEMINAR ROOM AND EQUIPMENT
Make arrangements to be admitted at least one hour early. (Don't
assume the room will be open).

Check tables and seating. Do I prefer
        ___ classroom style? ___ theatre style? ___ semicircle?

Is there a podium? _____

Check required audiovisual equipment:
___ Opaque projector
___ Overhead projector
___ Slide projector
___ Movie projector
___ VCR
___ Audiocassette player/recorder
___ Flip Chart (magic markers)
___ Blackboard/Whiteboard (chalk or markers)
___ Computer and large monitor
___ Other _____

Bring a "tool kit" that includes:
___ Scissors
___ Scotch tape
___ Thumb tacks
___ Pocket knife
___ Extra paper
___ Extra pens
___ Paper clips
___ Stapler
___ Other _____

- Advertising, "getting the word out," is probably the single most important aspect of running a successful seminar. The second is preparation.

- Seminars have a lot more "give and take" than speeches. Be prepared to tack things up, create handouts on the spot, to act spontaneously.

NEW SALES-BUILDING SEMINAR!

HOW TO BUILD CUSTOMER LOYALTY AND REPEAT BUSINESS

- Did you know that 96% of your unhappy customers will never complain to you...will never come back to your company...but many will bad-mouth you to as many people as possible?
- Did you know that it costs 5 times as much to get a new customer as it does to keep an old one?
- Did you know that customer service is frequently the difference between making money and losing money?

Attend the seminar that helps you and your employees understand what your customers want and how you can give it to them. Learn how to hire for excellence... train for service...measure for results.

Thursday, June 30
9:00 a.m. - 4:00 p.m.

Attendance is strictly limited. Reservations only. Seminar will be held at the Sylk Auditorium, Stamford, CT. $185 per person. Discounts available for multiple attendees from the same company. For information and reservations, call:

203-555-1800

Another value-packed seminar by

Relationship Associates

918 Gardner Street
Stamford, CT 06925

Phone:
203-555-9191
Fax:
203-555-9192

- Don't make people guess what the ad is about. Label it as a seminar.

- Phone calls draw impulse buyers. Make the number prominent.

"The rewards I've gained in learning about money management have been impressive, to say the least. Thank you."
Charles Robinson

If you have the sincere desire to be a financial success, dial 1-800-555-7979 and reserve your place in...
JOE LaROCCA's FINANCIAL FREEDOM WORKSHOP!

- Increase your income
- Enjoy the lifestyle you want
- Reduce your financial dependence on other individuals and institutions
- Build confidence in yourself and your future
- Master your personal finances

"I'm no longer afraid of investing; I now have the knowledge and confidence to make smart decisions in building my portfolio."
Sheila Lavin

Joe LaRocca's Personal Guarantee:
If you work with me, do all the exercises I give you, complete all the worksheets as directed, I guarantee that you'll create a financial action plan that will enhance your income and lifestyle beyond <u>their current boundaries...or your money back.</u>

By enrolling in this much-acclaimed seminar program, you'll learn Joe LaRocca's secrets for financial success. Call now because space is severely limited.

ONE-DAY ONLY!
First Penn National Bank
2nd floor meeting room, 9:00 a.m.-4:30 p.m.
Saturday, September 15

CALL 1-800-555-7979 or send the coupon below!

Mail to: Joe LaRocca Institute/412 Lavorett Ave.
Birmingham, AL 35247

"Joe LaRocca has helped me to lead a life of financial security."
Martin Moore

☐ **YES!** Enroll me in Joe's September 15 Financial Freedom workshop for just $295.
Method of Payment:
☐ Check/Money Order (payable to Joe LaRocca's Financial Success, Inc.)
☐ Charge my credit card:
   ☐ VISA ☐ Mastercard ☐ American Express ☐ Discover

Credit Card # _____

Exp. Date _____ Signature _____

Name _____

Address _____

City _____ State _____ Zip _____

Telephone _____

Did you indicate method of payment? No enrollment can be accepted without payment.

- Use testimonials if appropriate.

- If space is limited, sell the benefits of attending, as opposed to describing what goes on in the seminar.

ARTICLE PROPOSAL WORKSHEET

1. What is the subject of your article?
   _____
   _____

2. Explain why the article will be of benefit to the journal/magazine/
   newspaper readers:
   _____
   _____
   _____
   _____
   _____

3. Summarize the article (100-200 words):
   _____
   _____
   _____
   _____
   _____
   _____
   _____
   _____

4. Projected length of the article. How many words or double-spaced
   manuscript pages will there be?
   _____

5. Length of time required to write article: _____

6. Attach a resume (no longer than 2 pages). Emphasize your
   credentials relative to the subject of the article. If you've had other
   articles, features, or books published, mention them and enclose
   copies.

- The "benefit to the reader" segment is what will sell your article. If you can't make the editor understand how it will help the readers, it won't be published.

- If the proposal is accepted, you'll be advised of any fee schedule; you don't have to ask.

BOOK PROPOSAL WORKSHEET

Divide your proposal into three sections:

I. A 2- to 3-page, double-spaced section that clearly defines:

    A. The target audience. For whom is the book written?

    _____

    _____

    _____

    B. Reader benefits. What will happen to the reader as a result of
       reading the information you provide?

    _____

    _____

    _____

    C. The competition. What books have been recently published
       covering the same subject matter?(include title, author, publisher,
       copyright date)

    _____

    _____

    _____

    D. How does your book differ from the competition?

    _____

    _____

    _____

E. The projected length of the book. How many printed pages or double-spaced manuscript pages will there be?

_____
_____
_____

F. How many (if any) illustrations, charts, tables, graphs, etc., will there be?

_____
_____
_____

G. Estimated completion date of your manuscript.

_____

H. Marketing information. What professional, business, industry, fraternal, organizations/associations would be interested in your material?

_____
_____
_____

II. Include a detailed outline of each chapter (No less than 100-200 words per chapter).

III. Attach a resume (no longer than 2 pages) giving your educational and professional background, emphasizing any information that would provide credentials for your writing this book.

• Fill in all sections of this outline. It will provide publishers with the information they will need to properly evaluate your book concept.

• Neatness counts. A sloppy document will probably be discarded.

Company Name
Address
City, State Zip

Contact: Jim Whelan   Date
            (913) 555-1133

FOR IMMEDIATE RELEASE

PDI AND DIDACTICS MERGE
TO FORM NEW CONSULTING FIRM

Mission, KS—PDI, a labor relations consulting firm specializing in contract mediation, and Didactics, Inc., a management and organizational development consultant, have agreed to merge as of October 1.

Jim Whelan, Executive Vice President of the newly formed company—Universal Management—said that the merger "allows us to take advantage of our complementary skills and client base. We will now be able to service the broad spectrum of business, industry, and government from union and management perspectives."

Kerri Leyland, formerly president of PDI, will assume the role of managing partner. The new company will be located at 400 Renaissance Center Court, Mission, KS 66202 (913-555-1133).

- 30 -

- News of a merger or acquisition has a good chance of being published in a local newspaper's business section, regional business magazines, and industry publications.

- Include a quote from one of the parties about the benefits of the merger.

Company Name
Address
City, State Zip

Contact: Peg Morgan   Date
          (908) 555-0448

FOR IMMEDIATE RELEASE

WRITING CONSULTANTS PUBLISH NEW TRAINING PROGRAM

Piscataway, NJ—A new business writing course has just been published by PCI, Inc., a New Jersey-based training and course development firm.

THE WRITE WAY was designed to be used as an independent learning course to reduce the amount of time and lower the cost of classroom training. The course includes four audiocassettes, a 166-page workbook that includes numerous exercises, and a 40-page grammar guide that covers common areas of misuse by business people.

The course developers are Gerald Corliss and Paul Reston, partners in Power Communications, Inc., a consulting firm specializing in management training. Their seminars have helped train employees in more than 60 corporations and government agencies. They are also co-authors of books on grammar, writing and communication skills.

THE WRITE WAY sells for $79.95. Descriptive literature is available from PCI, Inc., 92 Arrowhead Drive, Piscataway, NJ 08854 (908-555-0448).

- 30 -

- Business publications are always on the lookout for new product releases. You'll enhance your chance of being published if you include an 8 x 10 glossy photograph with the press release.

- If you give an address where readers can obtain literature, it will often be included in the release.

Company Name
Address
City, State Zip

Contact: Daniel Breland   Date
(312) 555-2100

FOR IMMEDIATE RELEASE

LOCAL BUSINESS CONSULTANT SELECTED
TO HEAD UNITED HANDS FUND DRIVE

Chicago, IL—Daniel Breland, a Chicago-based time management and productivity consultant, will head this year's United Hands Fund Drive.

Called the "most ambitious undertaking in the history of Chicago fundraising" by alderman Henry Tilton, the $120,000,000 goal must be met to continue the 100% funding of many local charities, including public day care centers and senior citizen recreational facilities.

Mr. Breland stated that Chicagoans "will prove their generosity once again, and area businesses will play more of a role than ever before." Breland predicted that United Hands will exceed its unprecedented goal.

For information about volunteering, contact Daniel Breland, 4322 West Borden Street, Suite 601, Chicago, IL 60606 (312-555-2100), or call United Hands headquarters at 312-555-0090.

- 30 -

- Combine a release like this with a personal note to current and potential clients, asking if anyone in their organizations can help. You'll gain a higher profile, and you'll probably receive assistance.

- If you send a photo with a release (8"x 10" glossy finish is preferred by editors), be sure to caption it with relevant information (e.g., Business consultant Daniel Breland selected to head United Hands Funds Drive).

Company Name
Address
City, State Zip

Contact: Bert Connors   Date
          (215) 555-3330

FOR IMMEDIATE RELEASE

FAIR MATCHES ENTREPRENEURIAL HOPEFULS
WITH BUSINESS OPPORTUNITIES

Philadelphia, PA—The inaugural Entrepreneurs' Fair, held March 13, 14 and 15 at the Philadelphia Civic Center, attracted 55 companies seeking entrepreneurs, as well as thousands of potential entrepreneurs interested in business opportunities.

Most of the exhibitors were food and service companies seeking franchisees.

Bert Connors, president of Connors Venture Corp., located in Philadelphia, stated, "Our job is to match companies with entrepreneurs. And what better way than to bring them together in a buying and selling atmosphere?"

Jack Weymouth, an entrepreneur from Cherry Hill, NJ, said, "This concept is wonderful. Instead of having to contact dozens of companies for information, Connors has compressed the process into this two-day event. I'd recommend it to anyone wanting to start a business."

Connors expects the Entrepreneurs' Fair to become an annual event in the Philadelphia business community.

Interested exhibitors can contact Connors Venture Corp. at 300 Wayland Blvd. in Philadelphia (215-555-9988).

- 30 -

- Headlines can help attract an editor's attention. But be certain that your headlines are relevant.

- Try to get your company's name, and yours, mentioned throughout the release, so that regardless of where the release may be cut, your name will still appear.

Company Name
Address
City, State Zip

Contact: Lois Garner   Date
          (414) 555-8945

FOR IMMEDIATE RELEASE

NEW LIGHTING CUTS EMPLOYEE ABSENTEEISM

Milwaukee, WI—Walker Enterprises has boosted employee productivity by 28% in the third quarter. Harrison Woolrich, president and CEO, credits most of the improvement to enhanced office lighting. Walker Enterprises' new lighting program was engineered by office systems consultant Lois Garner of Office Productivity Management.

By scientifically combining "ambient" or natural lighting with "task" or specific job lighting, Ms. Garner has helped Walker dramatically decrease the incidence of eyestrain, headaches, and stress-related absences. According to Mr. Woolrich, better lighting has led to happier, more productive employees.

The new lighting program has another benefit: long-term cost reduction. Mr. Woolrich said that numerous studies show that the less expensive a lamp is to buy, the more expensive it is to operate. He also said that in addition to improved productivity, the company's new lighting program is estimated to deliver an energy savings of "no less than $25,000" over the next eight years.

Questions about the Walker Enterprises program may be directed to Ms. Garner at Office Productivity Management, 1181 W. Main Street, Wauwatosa, WI (414-555-8945).

- 30 -

• Aim for an opening sentence that will help an editor make a decision to "go" with your story.

• Make the client's success the focus of the story, but be sure to include your name, address and phone number.

Company Name
Address
City, State Zip

Contact: Grace Lee   Date
          (617) 555-3922

FOR IMMEDIATE RELEASE

DR. LAURA FREDERICKS NAMED TO SATELLITE TEAM

Boston, MA—Well-known aerospace and electronics consultant Dr. Laura Fredericks has been added to the staff of the Satellite Telecommunications Project, commissioned by the government of Syria.

According to Mohammad Al Rhayid, spokesperson for the Syrian Communication Consortium, "Dr. Fredericks' vast experience as a materials engineer consultant and her work in process failure analysis add a key component to the aerospace team assembled to launch Syria's first communications satellite."

Dr. Fredericks, who holds a dual degree in physics and mathematics from Duke University, has been involved in 15 communications satellite programs, offering consulting expertise in the area of conformal coatings, finishers, printed wiring boards, structural composites, and thermoset and thermoplastic materials.

Dr. Fredericks has been the recipient of numerous honorary awards for her performance on aerospace projects such as InterCom, MERLI, WEAL TV, AF3G, and Communiset.

- 30 -

- Ask the organization that hired you to issue a press release about your appointment. Be sure to provide suggested copy to insure that the release conveys the desired image.

- Even if you have to do it yourself, be sure that a release is issued to your local media, chamber of commerce, and any other organizations that may have potential clients. Tailor the release to the particular audience.

Company Name
Address
City, State Zip

Contact: Debbie Horan   Date
           (219) 555-5355

FOR IMMEDIATE RELEASE

HOW LONG WILL YOUR SAVINGS LAST?
FREE WORKSHOP, SUNDAY MAY 9, 2:00-5:00 P.M.

South Bend, IN—The Western Methodist Church is offering a free workshop for anyone who aspires to a comfortable and carefree retirement.

Lifestyle and retirement planning consultant Debbie Horan says that people are apprehensive about their financial security but, traditionally, do very little about it. She says "Retirement is a difficult transition even for people who have prepared for it. It's traumatic for those who haven't. Ideally, people should start the planning process in their 20's, not their 50's."

The "How Long Will Your Savings Last" workshop will guide participants through an audit of their assets and liabilities, and offer strategies for organizing, analyzing and evaluating their financial future.

To register for this valuable workshop, call or write Martha Vendergrift, Western Methodist Church, 670 Southland Street, South Bend, IN 46628 (219-555-3845). Enrollment is open until May 2, and there is no charge.

- 30 -

- Words such as "free" and "new" attract attention. A free seminar, for example, will be perceived by an editor as being a benefit to the public. Chances are good that the press release will be carried in your local newspaper.

- Headlines are often chopped or rewritten by editors. Repeat any important information from the headline in the body of the release.

Company Name
Address
City, State Zip

Contact: Leonard Harrison   Date
          (206) 555-7722

FOR IMMEDIATE RELEASE

ALBERT MOORE NAMED MAN OF THE YEAR

Bothell, WA—Financial consultant Albert Moore, president of Moore Management, Inc., has been given the coveted Man of the Year award by the Washington State Association of Financial Managers.

Mr. Moore has been a vocal leader in the fight to redefine an ethics code for financial consultants and managers. His 112-point report has been hailed as a landmark by the state Better Business Bureau and the Seattle Consumer League.

At a dinner held in his honor, Harry Vernon, Executive Director of the Association of Financial Managers, called Mr. Moore "an inspiration to financial consultants and their clients." Mr. Moore was lauded as a person of great personal integrity.

Albert Moore and his wife, Arlene, live on Court Street in Bothell, where they are active in community and school affairs. The Moores have two children: Amy, 9, and Peter, 11.

- 30 -

- Press releases for local newspapers, such as this one, should contain information about the individual's family, which editors consider of interest to readers.

- Whenever possible, use quotes in the release. They make the article seem more like a news story.

Company Name
Address
City, State Zip

Contact: Henry Watkins   Date
          (602) 555-3451

FOR IMMEDIATE RELEASE

"DEALING WITH CONFLICT" TO HIGHLIGHT
JUNIOR CHAMBER OF COMMERCE MONTHLY MEETING

Phoenix, AZ—Noted business consultant Henry Watkins will be the featured speaker at the June 26 luncheon meeting of the Phoenix chapter of the Junior Chamber of Commerce. The luncheon, scheduled for 12:00 noon in the main ballroom of the El Mesta Hotel, will precede the talk.

According to Mr. Watkins, managers' and supervisors' conflict-solving skills must be improved if American business is to remain competitive under the weight of a culturally diverse and changing workforce.

Participants will learn (1) how to assume responsibility for solving conflict, (2) methods for uncovering, defining, and discussing problems, and (3) techniques to set goals and create an action plan to minimize the impact of conflict.

Non-members are welcome. For reservations, call Rita Johnson, at 602-555-2877. Tickets are $35.00 if paid in advance, $50.00 at the door. Business students may register at half price (proper ID required).

- 30 -

• Keep your headline to one or two lines.

• Tell readers what they have to gain by attending. Don't assume that the title of the talk will stand on its own.

Company Name
Address
City, State Zip

Contact: Anthony Salese   Date
213-555-2200

FOR IMMEDIATE RELEASE

NEW MARKET RESEARCH HELPS PUBLISHER
CUT COSTS, REDUCE ADVERTISING RATES

Los Angeles, CA—Encore Publishing, owner of Nation's
Schools and Nation's Colleges, has merged the magazines into
one. The new publication is called Nation's Schools and Colleges.

Based on research conducted by Anthony Salese of Educational Directions, combining the magazines will provide a much
more cost-effective method of reaching school and college
facilities managers.

"A building is a building," says Salese, "whether it's an
elementary school or a college science lab. The sophistication
may vary, but both require tables, chairs, desks, restrooms,
blackboards, cleaning supplies, windows and ventilation."

Instead of requiring advertisers to purchase ads in two
magazines to reach both school and college facilities managers,
they now need to purchase only one. Roy Cohill, publisher of the
newly combined publication, says that the production and postage
savings will be passed directly to advertisers, creating the lowest
cost per thousand readers in the field.

Free copies of the research are available from Anthony
Salese, Educational Directions, 271 W. Agosto Avenue, Los
Angeles, CA 90101 (213-555-2200).

- 30 -

- This headline is tailored to magazines and newsletters that reach the advertising
  community. Think about your market before writing the press release.

- Offers of free research data will usually be printed. It's a good way to get your name
  and address published.

MANAGEMENT PLUS

Volume 3, Number 6 A publication of the Hodge International Management Group **December 1996**

Sales Management

Tips for Improving Telemarketing Sales

How many times have you listened to a telemarketing sales pitch that bored you from the first word? Most people admit that they've *never* heard an interesting pitch in their lives...that the phone caller always sounds as though they are reading from a script (which, of course, they usually are!).

Chances are, *your* telemarketers are boring your prospects, as well. And it probably frustrates you that all those leads you generate, all those dollars you spend to provide names to your telemarketing department, aren't being used nearly as effectively as they should be.

One of our clients was calling trucking firms to try to get them to sign up for a government-mandated drug testing program. Here's the way they greeted prospects:

"Hello. I'm from Atlas Drug Testing, and I'm responding to your request for information about our drug awareness and compliance program. Our program is now administered to 251 companies in the Pacific Northwest, including provision of all phases of gender-oriented, trained collection site personnel and evaluation of specimens only through N.I.D.A.-certified laboratories."

Is that opening factual and correct? Absolutely. Is it deadly dull? Absolutely. Even though someone who requested information should understand what was being said, there's no *involvement* in what was

• continued on Page 2

TIME MANAGEMENT BRIEFS

5 Tips for Cutting Meeting Time

1. **Always work from a written agenda.** Just as you wouldn't take a driving trip without a road map, you need to set a course for your meetings. And keep the agenda visible at all times, to keep people on track.
2. **Set a starting and an ending time.** Put pressure on people to arrive on time...and to complete the agenda in a specific time frame. When people know you mean business, they'll respect your time constraints.
3. **Don't hold regular meetings.** Very often, the weekly Monday morning review meeting is nonproductive and a colossal time-waster. Schedule meetings when they are necessary, not as exercises in hand-holding.
4. **Hold your meetings standing up.** You can't believe how quickly things can be accomplished when no one is seated and comfortable.
5. **Send notes instead of holding meetings.** If the basic reason for a meeting is to pass along information, why make people spend time in that meeting? Write the information and send it to whoever needs it.

Time Management Quotes:

"Time is the scarcest resource, and unless it is managed nothing else can be managed."

—Peter Drucker

"There can't be a crisis next week. My schedule is already full."

—Henry Kissinger

"People who make the worst use of their time are the same ones who complain that there's never enough time."

—Various Bosses

Management and Communication

Negotiation Checklist

There may be no activity that requires better communication skills than negotiating, which is one of the prime management prerequisites. To be a top negotiator, you must be an active listener so you can identify the other party's interests, offers, and objections...and you need to be an excellent presenter so you can clearly communicate your own interests without offending the other party or giving up too much. Here's a negotiating checklist you should review, whether you're dealing with a subordinate, a vendor, a labor negotiator, or your boss:

1. Show respect for the other party, even if you disagree with their position.
2. Keep your emotions under control. When you're emotional, you don't function as well.
3. Don't use sarcasm, even in jest.
4. Appear confident. Speak with a firm voice.
5. Sit erect at all times and maintain eye contact.
6. Speak in specifics. Avoid generalities. (For example, don't say "many," or "a lot"; give specific numbers.)
7. Be direct without being offensive.
8. Be careful of how you use the words "Why" and "You." They often sound like blaming words.
9. Make requests, not demands.
10. Pay attention to the speaker.
11. Read others' body language to see if you're getting through to them.
12. Use body language to show you're listening.
13. Use questions to get information and to control the conversation.
14. Don't interrupt.
15. Always clarify and restate what's been said to be sure that what you heard is what was said.

DEALING WITH CHANGE

Recognizing When to Change: Product Life Cycles

There are four stages in any product's life cycle: (1) introduction, (2) growth, (3) maturity, and (4) decline. These stages are as inevitable as night and day. But many firms, particularly small and entrepreneurial firms, don't plan for this very natural progression. And the lack of planning dramatically affects not just performance...but survival.

By recognizing what evolutionary stage you're in and planning to meet changing conditions and requirements, you will have gone a long way toward ensuring continuity and success. One specialty ad agency, for example, found that competition and in-house agencies were whittling away at their sales. They bought a print shop and created an advertising premium line that reinvigorated the business.

A housing contractor dramatically improved his business by *reducing* his firm's size, refusing to bid on increasingly expensive tract homes, and concentrating on the custom home market. A chicken processor fought her way back into a very mature market by adding game hen to her line.

What's important to note is that none of these examples were spur of the moment decisions. Business trends were recognized, evaluated, and planned for.

Did you notice the overriding thread in each of these companies? They all found success by sticking with what they already knew. They capitalized on products that could be integrated into their marketplaces.

For more information on product evolution, call Harvey Williams at 301-555-2724.

MANAGEMENT PLUS

is published bi-monthly
as a service of the
Hodge International Management Group
1422 W. Milbury Street
Baltimore, MD 21201
Phone: 301-555-2720
Fax: 301-555-3731

For additional copies or for more information, call or write Betty Antonelli.

MANAGEMENT PLUS is a management consulting firm serving the growth challenges of small businesses.

• *continued from Page 1*

being said. A good telemarketer can learn how to draw a prospect into a *two-way* conversation. Here's how Atlas switched pitches...and achieved a 200% increase in conversions:

Atlas: Hello. I'm glad you requested information about improving your drug compliance program because the government has cracked down so hard recently, that companies who thought they were covered have been fined for noncompliance. Let me ask you a question before I answer yours: Have you ever had a government audit of your driver drug plan?

Client: No.

Atlas: That's good. But that means the chances are better than 1 in 3 that you *will* be audited this year. Let's make sure that you're ready for it. Do your specimen collection procedures follow Health and Human Service guidelines?

Client: I think so. Would you refresh my memory?

Atlas: I'll do better than that. I'll send you a list of the guidelines because anything you're *not* doing could earn you a substantial fine. But let me ask you another question: Are you familiar with chain of custody documentation? That seems to be a missing detail that's costing a lot of companies major disruptions and penalties.

The new telemarketing script took advantage of the fact that many company drug administrators are not technical experts and had been sold by the first company that called on them. While it's difficult to come out and say that a competing company is incompetent, it's easy to demonstrate what's missing from their service. Fear of noncompliance is a powerful motivation in this particular field.

Questions are a key to successful telemarketing. You can't draw people out by talking at them. Virtually everyone will respond to questions. If the prospect had responded with a "yes" instead of a "no" the telemarketer would have responded with: "I'll bet you're not looking forward to going through that again. What did they find needed improvement?" Then the pitch can address specifics.

For information about telemarketing, contact our senior telemarketing consultant, GeorgAnn Williams at 301-555-2722.

• When creating a newsletter, concentrate on those areas in which your consulting practice specializes. Demonstrate your expertise through success stories, not through self-serving statements.

• It's worth the investment to pay a writer to compile your newsletter. Poor grammar and dull writing will not enhance your image.

Interviewing Prospects 6

Interviewing prospective clients provides the opportunity to accomplish several critical objectives: to find out what the client wants, to impress the client with your professionalism, and to determine whether the client and the project are something you're interested in pursuing. This process is called "qualifying the prospect," and there are a number of specific techniques you can use.

Qualifying the Prospect

Use every Request for Proposal (RFP) as an opportunity to qualify a prospect. Collect as much information as you can from the prospect before you begin writing the proposal so that you can make an informed decision about the viability of the request.

There are a number of specific questions you will want to consider:

- **What is the nature of the project?**
  Does the assignment match your expertise? Is it something you'd feel comfortable handling?
- **What is the scope of the project?**
  Is it a bigger or longer assignment than you are accustomed to accepting? Will you need additional help and is that help available to you?
- **What is the urgency of the project?**
  Will you have adequate time to do an effective job or will the prospect's time constraints force you to compromise your customary level of quality?
- **Has the prospect ever used consultants before?**
  If not, you may need to spend time helping your prospect understand how to work with a consultant. Although rarely a reason not

to proceed, it is good to be aware of the issue so that you can plan for it ahead of time.

- **Does the prospect have money budgeted for this project or a sense of how much your services will cost?**

  Better to ask the question now than wait until you have spent time writing the proposal. Often, the prospect will give you some general guidelines: "We're hoping we can keep costs under $25,000" or "If your bid comes in between $20,000 and $30,000, you will be in the ballpark."

  Sometimes, depending on the rapport you have developed with the prospect, you may even get much more specific information: "We had one consultant last year who quoted us a figure of $60,000; that was twice as much as we had planned to spend for this kind of project."

- **How many other consultants or firms have been asked to submit proposals?**

  The answer to this question may help you decide whether the prospect is simply collecting data for a resource file, planning to use the ideas of a number of consultants to design an internal solution, or going through the motions of soliciting and collecting proposals to meet some arbitrary requirement before giving the assignment to someone who is already "wired" to the company.

  Most companies will narrow the field to a handful of choices (3 to 5) before asking a consultant to submit a proposal. Those are good odds, especially if the prospect assures you that some preliminary screening has already been done, perhaps based on previous discussions with you, conversations with other companies or consultants, your reputation in the field, or your marketing materials.

- **How will the prospect use your proposal?**

  If the prospect says that your proposal will be reviewed by a task force or committee, ask for more specific information so you can tailor your proposal to that audience and use language that is appropriate to your readers. For example, a CEO may expect only a summary of key points, while a Vice President of Engineering may want a detailed, step-by-step outline and process schedule.

- **How will a decision be made: by whom and when?**

  Once again, the answer should give you some idea about the urgency and importance of the project, as well as helpful information about the style of the proposal you are planning to write.

- **Will you have an opportunity to discuss your proposal with**

others or to make a formal presentation to the ultimate decision makers?

Some type of verbal review or formal presentation is always more desirable than letting the outcome depend solely on the written word. Even your best proposals can benefit from an opportunity for you to clarify and expand what you have put down on paper.

- **What are the most critical outcomes the prospect would like to achieve?**

Pay very close attention to the exact words the prospect uses so that you can repeat key phrases, word for word, in your proposal. One of the most important attributes of a good proposal is its ability to demonstrate that you have listened carefully to your prospect's assessment of the problem.

- **How will the prospect know if the desired outcomes have been achieved?**

Some companies will want to use "hard data" to measure the success of your consulting efforts: increased profits; reduced turnover; less time getting new products to market; fewer employee grievances or customer complaints; better systems or procedures in place; fewer errors, less waste, or better quality control.

Some companies may use "softer" measurement criteria: improved morale; better communication; less friction between key departments; greater acceptance of individual differences in a diverse work group; more effective managerial decision making and problem solving.

Although you may be more comfortable with the latter, more general criteria, it is usually better to define the expected outcomes more precisely and specifically. You may even help the prospect clarify bottom-line expectations by asking some probing questions like:

1. How will you know you have gotten a satisfactory return on your investment (ROI) for the money and time you are planning to spend on this project?
2. What will be different about the company as a result of this project? What would you like to be able to observe or point to as a measure of the project's success?
3. What will people around here be doing or saying differently as a result of this project? What behavioral changes are you expecting?
4. Suppose you were asked, "Are we better off now that the

project is over than we were before the consultant arrived?" What specific factors or improvements would you like to be able to mention?

- **What does the prospect see as the major obstacles to the success of this project?**
  It is important for you to know about potential problems, areas of resistance, or individuals who may not welcome or support your efforts. Worst case, the obstacles may be so significant that you may decide not to submit a proposal. Best case, you may be able to address some of these issues more directly in your proposal.

- **Is there a particular style or structure the prospect would like you to use in your proposal?**
  Sometimes, this question can produce a wonderful, unexpected outcome such as: "Why don't I show you (or give you) a copy of a proposal that a consultant gave us a few years ago. It's one that our president liked a great deal." Or you may learn: "Don't make it too long; under six pages would be ideal." Other information may shed some light on organizing your proposal: "We always prefer a one-page Executive Summary at the beginning; then you can go into much greater detail in the body of your proposal about methodology, scheduling, and costs."

  This is also a good time to ask about additional support materials. For example, would the prospect like a listing of all of your clients or would a few key references be preferred?

An Interview Questions form (6-01) is found later in the chapter.

Interviewing Techniques

In order to get the most information out of an interview, as well as to use the interview to impress the prospect with your professionalism, here are some basic rules to follow:

1. **Dress for success**. Top consultants don't risk being judged lacking because of inappropriate clothing. They wear conservative clothing, are well-groomed (clothing pressed, shoes shined, clothing lint-free), and maintain good posture whether sitting or standing.

   Although some industries are notoriously casual, give yourself a psychological edge by staying "in uniform."

2. **Be professional at all times**. During the interview, it's particu-

larly important to be perceived as a business-first consultant. To sell your image, you need to demonstrate that you:

- Have an open mind and are a good listener (see below)
- Are the kind of person with whom it would be enjoyable to work
- Are competent and well-informed

You don't want to be seen as someone who won't listen to an opposing point of view, or is nervous or excitable.

3. **Communicate effectively**. The information you gather at this meeting will be critical in your preparation of a proposal, if you choose to take that next step. Overcome communication roadblocks that could turn prospects off:

- **Mechanical Speaking/Droning.** The average listener becomes mentally passive when someone speaks without inflection or range of tone. Vary your tone and speed.
- **Inappropriate Body Language.** When a speaker's verbal message is at odds with their non-verbal message (e.g., smiling when discussing a serious problem). Be aware of your body language, and synchronize it to what you are saying—and look at your prospect when you speak.
- **Unorganized Message.** If the explanation is too long, and the topic isn't introduced properly, you'll lose your listener. Present your points in a logical fashion and summarize the main issues.

4. **Use both closed and open ended questions**. Asking the right questions is one of the primary skills of a consultant.

Closed ended questions—questions that answer WHO, WHAT, WHERE, and WHEN—are excellent for pinpointing basic facts. For example:

- Who will spearhead the engineering team?
- What is the goal of the reorganization?
- Would you do it again?
- Do you disagree with her position?
- Where will the training take place?
- When is the project due?

Open ended questions—questions that answer HOW and WHY—not only help you get into the process, they help keep the conversation flowing. While asking the question "Who will spearhead the engineering team?" may turn up a valuable name, you can gain more insight by following up with "Why do you think she's the right person to handle the job?"

Instead of asking, "Would you do it again?" you will get more information by asking, "How would you do it differently?" Instead of simply asking someone if he or she disagrees with a position, ask, "In what ways (HOW) do you differ from that viewpoint?"

Here are some questions that can be used in a variety of interview situations:

- If this occurs again, how will you handle it?
- What did you like most (or least) about...?
- What changes have occurred since...?
- You sound ambivalent about that. Can you explain what's keeping you from making a decision?

Questions will help you identify politically sensitive areas that should either be avoided or handled very carefully. Every organization has its own agenda and specific culture. If you fail to recognize either, you may never be considered for a project.

5. **Follow up**. There should be immediate written follow-up after the interview. In many cases, writing the proposal will take considerable time. Rather than lose the momentum of a successful meeting, send a letter to reinforce the relationship and build good will.

Once you have asked all the qualifying and informational questions, you'll be in a good position to decide whether you want to write a proposal for this particular prospect, and how to proceed with the proposal if you choose to do so.

If you decide not to submit a proposal, don't leave the prospect hanging. That's a sure way to not be asked to bid on future opportunities...and lose out on recommendations. A well thought out "no" marks you as someone of character and conviction. You'll only damage your chances of future business if you don't take the time to respond.

An Interview Checklist (6-02) and Communicating Checklist (6-03) are found later in the chapter. Follow-up letters (6-04 through 6-11) are located at the end of the chapter.

INTERVIEW QUESTIONS

Questions for you to answer:

• Does this prospect really want to do business with you?

_____

• Do you really want to do business with this prospect?

_____

• Will you get an appropriate return on your investment of time and energy by presenting a proposal to this prospect?

_____

• Is this "good" business for you?

_____

Questions for the prospect to answer:

• What is the nature of the project?

_____
_____
_____

- What is the scope of the project?

  _____
  _____
  _____

- What is the urgency of the project?

  _____
  _____
  _____

- When does the prospect want to receive your proposal?

  _____
  _____
  _____

- Has the prospect ever used consultants before to meet similar needs?

  _____
  _____
  _____

- Does the prospect have money budgeted for this project or a sense of how much your services will cost?

  _____
  _____
  _____

- How many other consultants or firms have been asked to submit proposals?

  _____
  _____
  _____

- How will the prospect use your proposal?

  _____
  _____
  _____

- How will a decision be made: by whom and when?

  _____
  _____
  _____

- Will you have an opportunity to discuss your proposal with others or to make a formal presentation to the ultimate decision makers?

  _____
  _____
  _____

- What are the most critical outcomes the prospect would like to achieve?

  _____
  _____
  _____

- How will the prospect know if the desired outcomes have been reached?

  _____
  _____
  _____

- What does the prospect see as the major obstacles to the success of this project?

  _____
  _____
  _____

- Is there a particular style or structure the prospect would like you to use in your proposal?

  _____
  _____
  _____

- If the prospect can't answer most of the questions adequately, you should think carefully about taking on the project.

- The more details you uncover in the interview, the greater the chance of writing a winning proposal.

INTERVIEW CHECKLIST

1. Dress for Success
   - Wear conservative, freshly pressed and cleaned clothing. Don't risk being judged poorly because of what you wear.
   - Shine your shoes.
   - Maintain good posture.

2. Be Professional at All Times
   - Keep an open mind. Let the prospect see that you are willing to consider all sides of an issue.
   - Learn about the company. Before you meet, check sources at the library (reference books, newspaper articles), local Chamber of Commerce, annual reports, employees. You'll impress any client with knowledge of the company's operation.
   - Be gracious and friendly, but don't clown around and risk being considered a lightweight.

3. Understand What the Client Wants
   - Determine the reason you're there. If you walk out of the interview without knowing what you are being asked to achieve, you can't be successful.
   - Determine what the fee range is. There's no sense in spending hours or days developing a proposal without having a sense of the payoff.

4. Communicate Effectively
   - Present your story clearly and listen carefully to the prospect.

5. Use Closed and Open Ended Questions
   - Questions help you gather information and solve problems.
   - Closed ended questions answer WHO, WHAT, WHERE, WHEN, and help you pinpoint names, places, dates, things, statistics, etc.

- Open ended questions answer HOW and WHY, and help you understand reasons and processes. They keep conversation flowing since they can't be answered with a yes or a no.

6. Establish the Need for Measurements
   - Good consultants insist on accountability. By establishing measurable parameters, you and your client will have a basis for evaluating results.

7. Take Notes
   - Show your client you're interested in what is being said.
   - Create a written record for future reference.

8. Follow-Up
   - Don't let a first meeting end without follow-up.
   - If the proposal can be sent quickly, it and the cover letter are your immediate follow-up.
   - If the proposal requires some work, be sure to send an immediate letter to thank, confirm, promise or summarize.

- Following a comprehensive checklist will assure that you handle all aspects of the interview properly.

- Practice sessions with friends are a valuable tool for honing your interviewing techniques.

COMMUNICATING CHECKLIST

Identify the roadblocks to effective two-way communication that are created by BOTH you and the listener:

- Mechanical speaking/droning
- Uncoordinated body language
- Unorganized message
- Not being prepared to listen
- Jumping to conclusions
- Emotional listening

Overcome the roadblocks by:

- Varying the tone and speed of your speech
- Matching body language to what you're saying
- Presenting your information in a logical sequence and summarizing key points
- Focusing on what your prospect is saying, not their mannerisms
- Being actively interested in the speaker
- Probing with questions when things are unclear
- Being business-like and supportive
- Putting aside emotional feelings to understand the message

Keep an interview going by:

- Using questions to encourage participation
- Giving information that is requested
- Minimizing your interruptions
- Reinforcing what is said

- Superior communications skills may earn you additional business. Work on your weakest areas to enhance your opportunities for success.

- Be aware that your prospect may have weak communications skills and be prepared to deal with them effectively.

Company Name
Address
City, State Zip

Date

Mr. Lorne Davis
President
Electrical Solutions
1301 Waters Lane
Louisville, KY 40297

Dear Mr. Davis:

Thanks for passing my letter on to Sally Carlson. She and I will be meeting on the 22nd, and I'm looking forward to offering a number of suggestions as to how Electrical Solutions can increase its share of government contract awards. I think you're just a step or two away from some large contracts.

I hope we have the chance to meet some day.

Cordially,

James Bardsley

- If you receive a downward referral (e.g., president to vice president), make it a point to (a) thank the person for the referral, (b) let them know that a meeting will take place, and (c) indicate that the meeting may prove significant to the company.

- Be positive about the benefits of working with you.

Company Name
Address
City, State Zip

Date

Mr. Allen Alesi
Wellington Industries
One Steel Master Way
Hollywood, FL 33019

Dear Mr. Alesi:

I appreciate the time you made available on the phone...and I particularly appreciate your willingness to talk about how Wellington Industries should be able to convert ancillary products into a major profit center.

I'll see you at 9:00 a.m. on Thursday, the 9th. I'll fill you in on why I think you should enter this market...and how it's possible to quickly turn a significant profit on ancillary products (with little cost or effort).

I'm looking forward to the meeting.

Cordially,

Natalie Rossen

- A short note should be sent to your prospect which (a) confirms the meeting, and (b) expresses enthusiasm.

- You can build a sense of anticipation with a "tease," a line or two that promises to disclose something of value. (Just be sure you can deliver!)

Follow-up Letter, Thank You for Meeting (6-06)

Company Name
Address
City, State Zip

Date

Mr. Eugene McLaughlin
Martin and Robinson, Inc.
535 N. Allison Street
Houston, TX 77170

Dear Mr. McLaughlin:

I'm not sure who said "Marketing is an attitude, not a department," but from what I saw at our meeting last week, it applies to your organization.

It's always a treat to work with companies that constantly reexamine and redefine their marketplace and strategies. If one of your new directions includes children's products, I have the expertise and contacts to help you make a major impact.

Thanks for the time, interest and opportunity. If you need any additional information, or if you'd like to toss around an idea or two before making a final decision, please feel free to call.

Looking forward to seeing you again.

Cordially,

Nelson Darling

- If the client isn't quite ready to request a proposal, don't be afraid to give yourself a gentle plug.

- Without fawning, make it clear that you understand and appreciate how much effort and intelligence your potential client is applying to a project.

Follow-Up Letter, Proposal Will be Sent (6-07)

Company Name
Address
City State Zip

Date

Joseph Manning, Ph.D.
Calumet College
1100 Horton Drive
Bristol, CT 06010

Dear Dean Manning:

As a former Dean, I'm aware of the dilemma in which you find yourself: You know there's funding out there, but you have neither the time nor the staff to go after it.

That's where I enter the picture. I can conduct the planning and related documentation activities that are required to take advantage of complicated grant application programs. As you'll see in the proposal you'll receive next week, I can incorporate these critical elements of Title III Institutions Grant Programs into your program:

- Long and short range goals
- Objectives
- Evaluation criteria
- Primary funding sources

I enjoyed the meeting and I'm looking forward to working with you. I know from past experience that we'll be successful in creating a database that will take advantage of many available grants. My proposal will be in your hands on January 12.

Sincerely,

Albert Tardell

- Create a sense of anticipation with a restatement of what you will do for the client.

- Lock yourself into a date and stick with it.

Company Name
Address
City, State Zip

Date

Ms. Alicia Hebron
Design Alternatives, Inc.
One Willow Way
Minot, ND 58704

Dear Ms. Hebron:

Here's a copy of the study you asked to see. I think it will give you (1) an overview of the enormous market for home renovation and remodeling, and (2) a sense of what I can bring to your proposed project.

I enjoyed having the chance to meet you and to gain insight into your company's ambitious plans for growth. Since I've helped guide a number of small companies through the land mines of expansion, I think our companies are a perfect match for each other.

I'll have my complete proposal to you by Tuesday, May 18.

Sincerely,

Carl Finnegan

P.S. Stan Warner, of the Independent Builders Association, agreed to let me send you this copy of the remodeling and renovation study I created for his organization. His only request is that it not be distributed outside of your department. And he said if you have any questions, you could call him at 701-555-4200, ext. 322.

• If you're just starting out and don't have a body of work from your own company, use material with which you were involved when you worked for someone else.

• Providing the prospect with the phone number of a reference to call indicates self-confidence, an important trait in the consulting business.

Company Name
Address
City, State Zip

Date

Mr. Michael Wysocki
Fortune Products, Inc.
12 Winding Way Drive
Las Cruces, NM 88002

Dear Mr. Wysocki:

I was impressed with your willingness to give so much of your
time, and your obvious grasp of your company's strengths and
weaknesses. Your candor will help me structure a very detailed
and to-the-point proposal.

Before I go much further, however, may I have your permission to
spend a few hours in your warehouse? If possible, I'd like to
speak with employees at certain points in the work cycle. This will
give me a handle on the attitude of the work force as well as their
perception of productivity issues.

Before you say "yea" or "nay," there are two points you should
consider: (1) there's no charge for this pre-proposal work, and (2)
this approach has been very helpful in the past. Hibbard Construction and Allied Software can attest to that.

I'll call you on Monday to get your positive (I hope) answer.

Sincerely,

Samuel Wilson

- Your willingness to put forth extra time in the proposal development stage may help
  you gain a job.

- Some consultants consider this kind of time billable. It's your decision whether the
  commitment is part of the cost of prospecting or if it should be built into the proposal so
  that you will ultimately be reimbursed.

Follow-Up Letter, Request for Time Extension (6-10)

Company Name
Address
City, State Zip

Date

Mr. Harold Buttress
Vanderbilt Aero Systems
4200 W. Garfield Street
Albany, NY 12257

RE: Proposal on feasibility of design, fabrication and
testing of LAPIC semicustom circuit option packages

Dear Harold:

Henry Ford once said, "Before everything else, getting ready is the secret to
success." He was right, of course. Preparation is the key to any successful
project...and that's why I'm requesting a two week extension (to November 15) on
the delivery of my proposal.

By extending the deadline, I'll have the time to pin down the work schedules,
systems access procedures, and several other conditions that may affect the
project. In retrospect, perhaps we were too anxious to get the project started to
think about all the variables that I had to deal with in constructing the proposal.

I'm sure you'll agree that it's preferable to push the proposal back an extra two
weeks to be certain that we don't fall into the no-man's land of cost overruns and
delays.

If you agree, will you sign the enclosed extension approval and return it to me?
I'll call to confirm your approval.

Cordially,

Leonard Iovino

- It's far better to ask for an extension than to hand in a proposal late. Be sure to support
  your request for more time with a legitimate explanation.

- Don't miss a deadline without permission. Many government contracts (as well as those
  from many companies) will not allow for even one minute's lateness.

Company Name
Address
City, State Zip

Date

Ms. Anne Harding
General Brands, Inc.
570 Lawrence Avenue
Louisville, KY 40290

Dear Ms. Harding:

Although the opportunity to participate in the development of corporate-wide assessment centers is attractive, the time frame you specified for submitting a proposal is shorter than I require. And rather than submit a document that shortchanges both of us, I'll withdraw my name from consideration.

While I'm not in a position to help on this project, may I recommend someone who can? Ian Jefferson of MetaPro has been instrumental in the success of a number of assessment centers, and has designed many validated assessment instruments. If you'd like to consider another proposal, I strongly suggest you call him at 502-555-0988.

Thanks again for thinking of me. I hope you'll consider me for future projects.

Sincerely,

Nadine Ammond

• It's better to back off a project than to do a poor job.

• You can be of value with a good recommendation. And your professionalism may help you get a project from the company next time.

Developing Proposals 7

Proposals are an integral part of a consultant's business development strategy. In some cases, a proposal may be the last step in the sales process, the culmination of your efforts to identify, clarify, and respond in writing to a prospective client's needs. In other cases, a proposal may be the first step in the process of introducing yourself and explaining your capabilities to a prospect.

Reasons Clients Ask for Proposals

Prospects request proposals for a variety of reasons. The most obvious one is to sort out the competition and make an informed decision about which consultant can best meet their company's needs at a particular time. This is a valid reason for asking the consultant to define how they would approach an assignment and to describe what makes them different from or better than others.

Another reason prospects ask for proposals is to make budgeting and scheduling decisions based on what they ultimately perceive as a viable solution to their problem. Their objective is to get a clearer understanding of certain criteria by asking the consultant to describe how long the proposed project would last, how much of the consultant's time and how much of their time would be involved, when the project would begin and end, and how much the consultant would charge for the work.

Prospects might also decide to collect information from a number of consultants to help them determine the best course of action to follow. This can be helpful to you if you ultimately get the assignment and are allowed to see the information the other proposals contain. Even if you don't get the assignment, your proposal may have made enough of a positive impression that the prospect will remember you for future business.

When a proposal is rejected, it's always good to ask why you were not chosen and to find out if you will be considered for other assignments. By asking these questions, you may get useful feedback about your fees, your methodology, the quality of your proposal, and the advisability of keeping in touch with this prospect.

Finally, some prospects may ask for a proposal knowing from the start that they have no intention of hiring an outside resource. Their real intention is to collect ideas about how to solve the problem themselves so that they can then design their own internal solutions. Although this is obviously a waste of your time and energy, it is also difficult to detect or prevent. Most good companies do not encourage or tolerate this practice.

Interviewing the Prospect

Before beginning the proposal writing process, be sure to review the Interviewing chapter (Chapter 6) which tells you what information you'll need, and how to extract it from the prospect, to write a winning proposal.

Proposal Objectives

As you begin to organize your thoughts, there are three overall objectives you should keep in mind. A good proposal demonstrates your understanding of the prospect's real needs; it documents your ability to provide services to satisfy those needs; and it provides a plan of action that will be implemented upon acceptance of your proposal.

These are the critical areas that you should cover in every proposal. Anything else you may want to include that does not contribute significantly to meeting these objectives should be kept separate, as part of your total package, but not as part of your actual proposal.

Structure your proposal so that it has minimum impact on your time and maximum impact on your prospect. Before we focus on writing the proposal, let's consider the proposal package.

To get an overall sense of the proposal writing process, refer to the Six Step Process for More Productive Proposals (7-01) and Systematic Approach to Proposal Writing (7-02) at the end of this chapter.

The Proposal Package

Most proposal packages have three major components :

- A cover letter
- The proposal itself
- Proposal attachments

The **cover letter** is usually a one-page document that summarizes:

- Why the proposal is being sent (solicited vs. unsolicited).
- What is in the package.
- Particular areas of emphasis that you would like to high-light.
- Any significant differences between what the prospect asked for (or what you said you would include) and what you actually have included.
- What you will do next.

The **proposal** itself is the most important part of the package. Its length depends on how much information you need to include to meet the three objectives stated earlier but, in any case, the shorter the better. It functions both as a sales tool and as a project planning document. Information should be presented in a logical, sequential way and should attempt to answer the prospect's most important questions:

- What will you do and why?
- How will you do it ?
- When will you do it?
- How much will it cost?

To cover these important details, effective proposals are often divided into three parts:

1. The first section, the **introduction**, provides an overview or summary. It usually includes the following:

   - Your understanding of the prospect's issues, needs and desired outcomes.
   - A summary of any previous conversations using the prospect's own words (to demonstrate that you listened well).
   - A brief description of the key areas you intend to address in the proposal, stated in terms of the prospect's objectives.

   A summary statement like: "It is my understanding that you are concerned about the following key project objectives" can help you make a smooth transition into the next section of your proposal.

2. The second section, the **methodology section,** is the heart of your proposal and should include:

- A more detailed description of how you propose to help meet the prospect's objectives, stated in terms of actions you will take, services you will provide, outcomes that will be achieved, and benefits to the prospect.
- Highlights of any unique services, techniques, procedures, programs or expertise that apply specifically to the prospect's defined needs and which help distinguish you from other consultants who may be competing for this project.
- A focused solution to the prospect's most critical problems that incorporates references to supporting material included in your proposal attachments.

This description of your recommended approach should lead into the last section of the proposal.

3. This section, the **timing and cost section**, should be realistic and specific. In addition to the quality of your approach (as described in the preceding section of the proposal), timing and cost issues usually weigh heavily in a prospect's decision-making process. Try to emphasize:

- Scheduling information, based on your ability to meet the prospect's time constraints as well as the impact the project will have on any of the company's internal resources (if any).
- Pricing information including "free" or "discounted" services and any options that are appropriate.
- A payment schedule that describes how you would prefer to be paid and when you anticipate submitting invoices to the client for both fees and expenses (retainer, monthly, progress payments at key points during the project, actual expenses when incurred, etc.).

4. The final (and optional) section of the proposal contains **proposal attachments**. Depending on the prospect's familiarity with your company, or for coworkers at the client's company who may need additional supporting documentation, you may want to include information that is kept separate from your actual proposal.

Remember to refer readers to these attachments either in your cover letter or in the body of your proposal. Here are the most common kinds of attachments:

- A description of your company: history, structure, size, philosophy.
- A biographical sketch highlighting your academic background and work history; special awards, certificates, or other forms of recognition; professional associations or affiliations; any published articles or books; any other accomplishments or successes directly related to your ability to meet the prospect's current needs.
- Current or recent clients, particularly those that have a specific application to the prospect's industry, size and need.
- Any special programs, methods, procedures, techniques, tools or materials that you can provide (described in detail if you have decided not to include this information within your proposal).
- Any additional information that you would like the prospect to read as part of the decision-making process: articles, testimonials, industry statistics, "success stories," letters of recommendation, etc.

Keep in mind that most prospects have neither the time nor inclination to wade through page after page of material. Keep your proposal as brief as you can, while covering the subject as thoroughly as you consider necessary.

A Proposal Development Checklist (7-03), Proposal Attachments Checklist (7-04) and Proposal Writing Checklist (7-05) are found later in the chapter.

Writing the Proposal

Write your proposal with your prospect's perspective in mind. Knowing what challenges the reader is facing, and what they need to accomplish, will help guide you in determining how you approach the proposal.

Use language that is as clear and concise as possible. Often, the biggest challenge is to "demystify" what you do, to step back from your area of expertise and use language that will make sense to a non-expert. Use words that will clarify rather than confuse, and keep an eye out for jargon or "insider terminology" that may not be widely understood.

When writing a proposal, use a style and tone that is conversational. In most cases, the person receiving your proposal will need to "sell" your ideas to someone else in the company: their boss, senior management, a task force, or the Board of Directors. So make an effort to use language that the reader can understand and repeat to others about what you are proposing to do.

Translate the features of your services into benefits for the prospect. Don't depend on your reader to identify the value of doing business with you. Spell out the benefits clearly throughout your proposal: "Taking this approach will produce the following results," or "This new product will help you maintain your reputation as a pioneer in the field," or "This procedure will help you accomplish your stated objectives on time and under budget." Make it clear that the company has a lot to gain by hiring you as a consultant.

Describing benefits can result in a number of other positive side-effects:

- It is a way to highlight the key sales points you want people in the company talking about after they have read your proposal.
- It is a way for you to define how you would like the company to measure the quality of your work during and after the project, thereby putting yourself in a position to help them justify the cost of hiring you.
- It puts you in a position to follow up later with the same company on much more familiar and comfortable terms: "Here's what I said you would get from the last project and here's what you got."

The ultimate question that most prospective clients probably ask themselves has less to do with your technical or professional ability than with your personal qualities and attributes. Although there is no empirical data to confirm this suspicion, our experience suggests that the final question always has something to do with trust: Does the consultant have credibility with me and with others in the company? Can our employees work well with this consultant? Will the consultant make me look good? Can I trust this person to be honest and to do a good job for us?

The more you can instill a feeling of confidence and maintain a personal rapport with your prospect through your proposal, the better your chances are of getting this assignment and possibly many more.

Keeping in Touch with Your Prospect during Proposal Writing

Although this practice is often overlooked or underestimated, there are many benefits to staying in touch with your prospect while you are creating the proposal:

- You can avoid making assumptions based on misunderstandings or misinterpretations.
- You can gather any missing information that you may not have collected or clarified in your earlier conversations.
- You can explore possible objections or obstacles that may not have occurred to you before you started writing the proposal.

- You can make sure you are still a viable candidate for the project, especially if you are concerned about meeting the prospect's timing or cost factors.
- You can ensure that the rules or requirements have not changed, which sometimes happens in competitive situations as proposals are presented by other consultants.
- You can maintain rapport with the prospect and any other key decision makers.
- You may be able to gather information offered by the prospect about your competition.
- You can test the viability of any creative options that you did not discuss in earlier conversations (especially any additional services that may make more sense now than they did originally).
- You can confirm in the prospect's mind the importance of this opportunity by letting him or her know "I do care" and "I do want your business."

If your prospect is local and you think a follow-up meeting would be beneficial, call to schedule some time together. Otherwise, a telephone conversation can be almost as effective. A general introductory statement can set the stage for more specific comments or questions:

"I've been working on your proposal and..."

- I had an idea that I wanted to run by you.
- I realized that we didn't talk about your equipment and tool inventory (or something else you forgot to ask about).
- I'm not sure I got all of the details on the role you want your technicians to play in this project (or some other aspect of the project).
- I've been reviewing your schedule and your cost projections, and I have a few concerns which I'd like to talk to you about.

A Prospect Follow-Up Checklist (7-06) is found at the end of the chapter.

Finalizing Your Proposal Package

After you've written the proposal, revise and finalize it by focusing on three self-evaluation criteria:

1. Have you addressed the prospect's major concerns in a way that clearly shows the benefits of awarding you the business?
2. Have you used a style and language that is clear, concise, professional and personable?

3. Have you enclosed all of the necessary supplemental information or attachments and are they clearly identified?

Review the entire proposal package one last time to make sure that all information is accurate and complete.

If you are going to make a proposal presentation, prepare materials based on the style of meeting preferred by your prospect. Some companies will request a formal presentation; others may want a more informal question-and-answer session. Most companies will want to have copies of the proposal ahead of time so that they can read it and prepare questions or reactions. It is always advisable to find out about the prospect's preferences before working on the presentation so you don't waste time preparing something that won't be needed—or neglect to prepare something that will be helpful in selling your prospect.

A Proposal Package Checklist (7-07) is found later in the chapter. Proposals and proposal cover letters (7-08 through 7-20) are located at the end of the chapter.

SIX-STEP PROCESS FOR MORE PRODUCTIVE PROPOSALS

1. Get as much information as you can from the prospect before you begin writing the proposal. (See Chapter 6 for advice about interviewing your prospects.)

2. Think of each proposal as a strategic marketing and planning tool that can help you in your sales efforts with other prospects and customers. Refer to A Systematic Approach to Proposal Writing (7-02).

3. Structure your proposal package so that it has minimum impact on your time and maximum impact on your prospect. Refer to the Proposal Checklist (7-03) and the Proposal Attachments Checklist (7-04).

4. Write the proposal from the prospect's perspective using style and language that is clear and concise. Review the Proposal Writing Checklist (7-05).

5. Keep in touch with your prospect during the proposal preparation process. The Prospect Follow-Up Checklist (7-06) will be helpful.

6. Review the entire proposal package to ensure that all information is current, accurate, and complete. The Finalizing Your Proposal Checklist (7-07) should be followed.

- Proposal preparation is a time consuming process. Since it's frequently the key to winning an assignment, be sure you follow these guidelines to make the work pay off.

SYSTEMATIC APPROACH TO PROPOSAL WRITING

- Call your prospect or client and suggest writing a proposal without being asked, especially if you are convinced that your proposal 1) can help them get a jump on the competition, 2) will provide a new service, program, or approach that might be of interest to them, or 3) can keep them current with other companies in their marketplace.

- Set up a system that will help make proposal development increasingly easy and less time consuming.

- Organize and maintain a file of support materials for all types of proposals.

- Track your proposal writing activities so that you can measure the time spent and results achieved.

- Concentrate your time on identifying your best prospects, defining their real needs, and then proposing realistic, cost-effective solutions.

- Regardless of the outcome, ask for feedback about your proposal. Capitalize on the "hits" and learn from the "misses."

- Try to think of at least one other potential prospect or current client who might also benefit from the services you have described in the proposal you have just finished writing.

- Keep a file of your proposals handy. As you build up the quantity, you'll find that you'll be able to take sections from several, modify them with the specifics of the new project, and have a first-rate proposal in far less time than starting it from scratch. And you'll be using proposals that have a successful track record!

PROPOSAL DEVELOPMENT CHECKLIST

PROPOSAL OBJECTIVES
- Demonstrate your understanding of the prospect's real needs.
- Document your ability to provide services to satisfy those needs.
- Provide a plan of action that will be implemented upon acceptance of your proposal.

THE PROPOSAL PACKAGE
1. Cover Letter

- Tell why the proposal is being sent (solicited vs. unsolicited).
- Describe how the prospect will benefit from the proposal.
- State what is in the package.
- Explain differences between what the prospect asked for and what you have included.
- Indicate what you will do next.

2. The Proposal .

The first section (Introduction) should provide an overview or summary focused on the context and scope of the whole proposal: problem, objectives, desired outcomes.

The next section (Methodology) is the heart of your proposal and should include a more detailed description of how you propose to help meet the prospect's objectives, stated in terms of actions you will take; services you will provide; outcomes that will be achieved; benefits to the prospect. This is your response to the questions: What will you do and why? How will you do it and why?

The last section (Timing and Cost) should be an accurate, realistic, and comprehensive assessment of the schedule and the costs of doing the work. This is your response to the questions: When will you do it? How much will it cost?

3. Proposal Attachments

Include any additional supporting documentation you may want keep separate from your actual proposal. See Proposal Attachments Checklist (7-04).

- Each part of the proposal is important. Spend the necessary time making each section as clear and complete as you can.

PROPOSAL ATTACHMENTS CHECKLIST

- A description of your company: history, structure, size, philosophy.

- Biographical material highlighting your academic and business background; special awards, certificates, or other forms of recognition; professional associations or affiliations; any published articles or books; any other accomplishments or successes directly related to your ability to meet the prospect's current needs.

- Current or recent clients that have a specific application to the prospect's industry, size, location, and need.

- Any specific programs, methods, procedures, techniques, tools, or materials that you can provide (described in detail if you have decided not to do so within your proposal).

- Any additional information that you would like the prospect to read as part of the decision-making process: articles, testimonials, industry statistics, personal "success stories," letters of recommendation, or other marketing materials.

- The attachments you prepare for proposals can be those you're already using to market your practice—and vice versa.

PROPOSAL WRITING CHECKLIST

- Write your proposal with your prospect's perspective in mind.

- Use language that is as clear and concise as possible.

- Demystify what you do.

- Avoid using jargon, buzzwords, acronyms, euphemisms, or words with specialized meaning.

- Use a style and tone that is as conversational as possible.

- Translate the features of your services into benefits for the prospect.

- Highlight the key sales points you want people in the company talking about after they have read your proposal.

- Define how you would like the company to measure the quality of your work during and after the project, thus putting yourself in a position to help them justify the cost of hiring you.

- Remember that professional writing can and should still reflect the writer's personality and warmth.

- Lead the reader to conclude that your are totally trustworthy and that your work will be of high quality.

- Proposal writing is an art that can be learned with practice. Knowing the basic rules helps the learning curve.

PROSPECT FOLLOW-UP CHECKLIST

Keep in touch with your prospect during the proposal preparation process. It will enable you to:

- Avoid making assumptions based on misunderstandings or misinterpretations.

- Gather any missing information that you may not have collected or clarified in your earlier conversations.

- Explore possible objections or obstacles that may not have occurred to you before you started writing the proposal.

- Make sure you are still a viable candidate for the project, especially if you are concerned about meeting the prospect's timing or cost factors.

- Be certain that the rules or requirements have not changed, which sometimes happens in competitive situations as other proposals are mailed in or presented by other consultants.

- Maintain rapport with the prospect and any other key decision makers.

- Gather information offered by the prospect about your competition.

- Test the viability of any creative options that you did not discuss in earlier conversations (especially any additional services that may make more sense now than they did originally).

- Confirm in the prospect's mind the importance of this opportunity by letting them know "I care" and "I do want your business."

- The difference between staying in touch with the prospect and not can be the difference between getting the assignment or losing it to a consultant who does stay in touch.

FINALIZING YOUR PROPOSAL PACKAGE CHECKLIST

- Decide what you want to include in your total package and where each piece of support material will be placed in the overall package.

- Finalize the actual proposal by focusing on three criteria:

  1. Have you addressed the prospect's major concerns or issues in a way that clearly shows the benefits of awarding you the business?

  2. Have you used a style and language that is clear, concise, professional, and personable?

  3. Have you enclosed all the necessary supplemental information or attachments and are they clearly identified in the body of your proposal?

- Review the entire proposal package one more time to make sure that all information is current, accurate, and complete.

- Write your cover letter describing what is in the package, how it is organized, any particular areas that you would like to highlight, and what you will do next.

- If you are going to make a proposal presentation, prepare materials based on the style of meeting preferred by your prospect.

- The final review is your last chance to be sure you've covered all the bases. Take the time to do it properly.

Company Name
Address
City, State Zip

Date

Mr. John C. Horan
Chief Financial Officer
Tamec Engineering, Inc.
123 Witt Boulevard, Suite 456
Philadelphia, PA 19101

Dear John:

After last week's meeting with the Regional Vice Presidents, Mike Morro gave me a copy of your new Strategic Business Plan. Thanks for keeping me posted about these challenging objectives.

Since I can appreciate that you are under the gun with some tight deadlines, I thought an immediate reaction might be helpful.

You may be surprised that I converted these thoughts into a proposal, especially since you didn't request a formal response. However, I thought this format would be the best way for me to spell out ways that I could be a useful resource to you in the next few months.

Feel free to circulate the enclosed proposal to other Senior Managers for their reactions or questions. I will be back in my office next Thursday. I'll plan on giving you a call as soon as I get back.

Thanks again for the useful update about your new strategic objectives.

Best regards,

Nolan Parks

- The easiest unsolicited proposal cover letter to write is one to a happy client, one who values the work you do.

- Be careful not to abuse the relationship. As with any proposal cover letter, spell out why you are writing—and what the client will gain.

PROPOSAL TO HELP ORGANIZE A
TROUBLESHOOTING TEAM

I. Context and Scope of Proposal

During the past three years, we have worked closely with Tamec Engineering, Inc. to support strategic expansion and to help you establish regional branch offices. This proposal outlines recommendations for follow-up activities to address a major priority identified by Senior Management in your current five-year Strategic Business Plan which Regional Vice President, Mike Morro, reviewed with us last week.

Specifically, this proposal will describe our willingness and abilities to assist Tamec in organizing a Branch Troubleshooting or Start-Up Team that can be sent into target areas to improve offices and create new ones.

The idea of a High Impact Troubleshooting Team ("HIT Team") developed during one of our recent problem-solving conversations. The following sections of this proposal describe in greater detail the methodology, timing and costs associated with this project.

II. Methodology

To create this "High Impact Troubleshooting Team," we will:

  A. Help develop operational guidelines for the team:

  • Mission and purpose of the team
  • Organizational position, power, and accountabilities
  • Differentiation between skills required for turnaround and start-up situations
  • Methodology for selecting target projects to ensure maximum utilization of the team
  • Definition of prescribed time-lines and benchmarks for team decisions and recommendations

B. Help develop a financial plan including:

- budget allocations
- an incentive program for the team
- projections of estimated return-on-investment

C. Assist with the evaluation and selection of team members. Our experience has shown that organizations typically select the wrong "action team" members: the obvious choice is usually not the best one. We would help you weigh opportunity costs as an important factor in team member selection.

D. Lead team meetings focused on four key factors:

1. understanding the delicacy of turnaround situations (balancing bottom-line and humanistic considerations)

2. evaluating existing personnel (applying consistent performance measurement criteria to avoid favoritism)

3. recruiting, interviewing, and hiring new personnel

4. orienting new team members

III. Timing and Costs

Although some of your other projects may have more pressing time deadlines, we agree with Senior Management's conclusion that this idea has the greatest potential value to the company. We estimate a total of 8 days of consulting time to help Tamec create and activate this proposed "HIT team." Based on our current daily fee ($1,000) and projected expenses in the range of $1,000 - $1,500, I estimate that this project will cost around $9,500.

IV. Next Steps

We are prepared to offer Tamec any or all of the consulting support described in this proposal. Since timing and costs are important considerations, we are prepared to examine scheduling and payment options that are equitable to both of our companies. We look forward to the opportunity to be of further service.

- Don't be shy about referring to the long-standing relationship in the beginning of the proposal. After all, it's what makes this proposal different from those the client may receive from other consultants.

- Let "inside information" about the company's workings (learned through years of service to the client) guide you through the major sections of the proposal—but don't cut corners. Make your proposal complete and professional, just as you would for any prospective client.

Company Name
Address
City, State Zip

Date

Mr. David S. Stasak
Marketing Director
Fergus Medical Systems
789 N. Linton Avenue
Windsor, NJ 08520

Dear Mr. Stasak:

By way of introduction, I am a local consultant who specializes in helping organizations improve their sales and marketing capabilities. Most of my clients are Fortune 500 companies who, like yours, recognize the importance of keeping current about emerging trends and new opportunities in their defined marketplaces.

Recently, several of my clients began to re-evaluate the way they have always structured and conducted their annual sales meetings. They realized, for the most part, that they were spending a great deal of money sponsoring events that had very little tangible return on investment. With my encouragement and assistance, a few of them made a radical departure from tradition and brought people together for a "working" conference. Since then, I have had continued success presenting similar programs to other companies, which is the reason for this letter to you.

To be honest, I did a little homework before drafting this letter. I know, for instance, that you usually have a September conference in Atlantic City and that salespeople are flown in from all over the country for sessions that start on Thursday and end with a dinner party on Friday night (leaving the weekend as an optional extension for anyone who wants to stay until Sunday).

Judging by these admittedly limited facts, I thought you might be interested in learning more about what other companies are doing to improve their annual sales meetings. I have enclosed a brief proposal which will give you a quick idea of my approach and my fees.

I will call toward the end of next week to see if you have interest in a further discussion. Meanwhile, if you have any immediate questions, please feel free to give me a call at (201) 555-9876.

Sincerely,

Daniel Paramonte

- "Cold" solicitations for assignments can become much "warmer" if you do some homework before writing to a prospect.

- Don't wait for the prospect to call you. Always take the initiative and follow-up your letter and proposal with a call.

PROPOSAL TO DESIGN AND FACILITATE
A MARKETING CONFERENCE

I. Context and Scope of Proposal

As one of the leaders in your industry, Fergus Medical Systems has an impressive reputation for developing and installing the latest Health Care software and data retrieval systems. However, if you are like many of your competitors, your current marketing and sales efforts are being adversely affected by:

- A decreasing number of viable new customers
- An increasing number of independent consultants who can afford to offer your prospects lower prices
- Veteran salespeople who are complacent about pursuing new business and are content simply to maintain old, established accounts
- New and inexperienced salespeople who are reticent to make cold calls or hesitant about closing a sale
- Internal friction between your department and other departments (like Customer Service, Research, and Production)

These are some of the issues that companies such as yours wish to address. Instead of treating your annual sales conference solely as a chance for regional salespeople to get together to share "war stories" and listen to Senior Management pep talks, I help clients design a two-day conference that has both an immediate impact and a long-term payoff for them.

My role is to provide the following professional services:

- Conference theme
- General sessions
- Small group and breakout sessions
- Schedule of events
- Learning materials
- Leader materials

At the conclusion of this conference, participants will:

- Leave with a positive feeling about themselves and about the company.

- Gain a better appreciation of the contribution each member of the company makes to the success of the other members.

- Commit to serving the interests of all team members by giving the optimum in time, energy, and focus to their job.

- Improve marketing skills by participating in a non-competitive team exercise focused on various aspects of the sales process including prospecting, making presentations, dealing with objections, and closing a sale.

II. Methodology

I create a comprehensive program that allows interdepartmental teams of reps and staff managers to understand various marketing techniques, then practice them in simulated sales situations with managers. The exercises conclude during the afternoon of the second day, at which time departmental teams meet to apply what they have learned during the conference to their specific unit goals and activities. Participants develop a personal and a group contract specifying individual and team commitments for the coming year.

During the comprehensive exercise, teams rotate leadership roles (so that each member has at least one opportunity to lead the group) and shared decision-making responsibilities in the following activities:

- Defining product features and benefits
- Identifying possible buyer objections
- Identifying prospects and qualifying leads
- Preparing a sales presentation
- Scheduling an appointment with a prospect

- Making the sales presentation
- Dealing with objections and negotiating for agreement
- Closing the sale

III. Timing and Costs

During a three-week period of time, I meet with managers and designated salespeople to gather information about the planned conference. In the following two weeks, I preview my design with them and then revise it for their approval. Finally, I attend the conference, deliver one of the key-note sessions, and keep the program on schedule for two days. I bill $ 15,000 for 10 days of consulting time at my daily rate.

IV. Follow-Up

At no additional charge to my client, I talk to participants during the following month and prepare a Status Report based on actual commitments and action plans each attendee created on the last day of the conference.

V. References

I've attached a list of companies for whom I've conducted similar projects. I believe you would find it helpful to hear how they evaluate the benefits of my services.

- Any proposal gains credibility if you can recount successes with other companies.

- Be sure to include a list of references in your proposal package.

Company Name
Address
City, State Zip

Date

Mr. David E. Williams
Senior Vice President
Andrews Pharmaceuticals, Inc.
Two Valley View Parkway
Atlanta, GA 55555

Dear Mr. Williams:

As you probably know by now, I met with Ken Kaleta last Wednesday to discuss assessments for up to 10 managers in the Research and Development Division. On Ken's recommendation, I am enclosing my proposal for your review.

I am confident that I can complete this project within the designated time period and close to (or under) budget. I also believe that my recommended approach will have credibility with the managers involved.

I mailed Ken a separate copy of my proposal so that he has time to review it before your meeting on Friday. If either of you has questions at that time, please give me a call. I will be in the office all day Thursday and most of Friday morning.

Sincerely,

Marian Andropoulis

- Make it clear that this is a solicited proposal. It will carry more weight than one that hasn't been solicited.

- If several people at the client are involved, be sure to send your proposal to each of them (including the senior executive), making sure that all know who have received copies.

PROPOSAL TO DEVELOP
MANAGEMENT ASSESSMENT PROGRAM

I. Scope of Proposal

On October 9, I met with Ken Kaleta of Andrews Pharmaceuticals to discuss your division's interest in management assessments. The proposed process would result in the formulation of individual development plans for 5 managers who report directly to Ken and up to 5 additional managers who report indirectly to Ken.

Based on my understanding of the situation, I am pleased to present this proposal describing the sequence of activities I would complete during a six-week period in order to arrive at specific development recommendations for each individual selected for these assessments. I am prepared to begin this project within the next four weeks so that it can be completed during the current calendar year.

II. Project Schedule

Planning Meeting
• Review and discuss with you competencies traditionally associated with management positions
• Identify competencies that may be unique to your management team or to certain individual members of the team
• Agree on a list of competencies to be included in the assessment
• Discuss, in greater detail, the background and performance histories of current (and potential) managers who will be included in the assessment study
• Discuss specific, individual problems or areas of resistance that may affect the assessments
• Plan a pre-assessment meeting to review methodology to be used and to schedule assessments

Design
- Create assessment methodology and activities based on information gathered during planning meeting (may include standardized instruments, observation of structured activities, interviews, and other demonstrations of desired competencies)
- Review the design with you for revisions and approval

Pre-Assessment Meeting
- Test the assessment methodology and instruments with Ken so that he is comfortable with the process
- Schedule individual assessments

Individual Assessments
- Conduct approximately four hours of assessment activities with each of Ken's direct reports (5) and the managers who report to them (5)
- Prepare individual development plans for each manager describing strengths and areas for improvement

Assessment Reviews
- present assessment findings (including individual development plans for each of the managers) to Ken and to the managers

III. Timing and Costs

Planning Meeting	1 day
Design	2 days
Pre-Assessment Meeting	1 day
Individual Assessments	8 days
Assessment Reviews	2 days
TOTAL	14 days

Based on my standard fee of $1,200 per day, I estimate the cost for this project will be $16,800 for fees plus all reasonable and substantiated out-of-pocket expenses such as telephone charges, postage charges, or photocopying costs. The total cost, therefore, should not exceed $ 17,500.

IV. Authorization

Upon written authorization from Andrews Pharmaceuticals, I will schedule our planning meeting and initiate this project as described.

I look forward to the opportunity to be of service.

- The structure of a proposal should be dictated by the kind of project under consideration, the proposal's readers, and what your objectives are. There is no need to lock yourself into one single format.

- Using bulleted items makes this proposal easy to read.

Company Name
Address
City, State Zip

Date

Mr. Sean Bennett
Vice President of Operations
Trimarco Electronics, Inc.
Valley Mall Drive
Philadelphia, PA 19105

Dear Sean:

After our recent telephone conversation, I thought about the problem we discussed and arrived at what I think may be a better solution. Although I still believe that my other client would be amenable to having several of your employees attend one of their workshops, I am not certain that this approach would meet your needs. In some ways, it might not be any better than sending someone off to an external training workshop.

I have outlined a different option on the following pages, one that would give your project managers some individualized attention while, at the same time, emphasize the importance of interpersonal and team effectiveness. I conducted a similar workshop a few years ago for Jim Gligor when he was organizing his group. Post-program feedback was very positive, and Jim later credited the workshop with helping his new team identify and resolve some significant conflicts. Although I would change content and approach somewhat for your smaller group, many of the tools and concepts would be the same. I am not sure what your relationship is with Jim, but I think he would give you an honest assessment of my work with his group.

If you like what I've outlined, I could pull things together quickly and be ready to start as early as August. I've also been thinking about making a "marketing trip" to Philly around that time, so I could combine that with a visit to see you, which would reduce your cost for my travel expenses.

I'll be back in my office on June 22 if you want to call to discuss this proposal.

Best regards,

Martin Chang

- A letter that seeks to shift from one approach to another must be handled tactfully to avoid insulting the client. Explaining the reason for the shift is critical.

- Offering to save the client travel expenses by combining the visit with other business can help to "sell" a project.

Company Name
Address
City, State Zip

Date

Ms. Kathleen Coleman
Edwards & Co.
300 Smalley Blvd.
Memphis, TN 38109

Dear Kathleen:

Shown below are my recommendations for an integrated approach
to management development initiatives at Edwards & Co.

As I stated during our meeting on Friday, I am confident that S & S
Associates can provide the following material to Edwards & Co. by
mid-December of this year:

1. A master copy of a Core Training Program for First Line
   Supervisors (5 days of training material, including
   Intersession Work).
2. A master copy of a Leader's Guide for this program.
3. All learning aids (including overhead transparencies, handouts, and flipchart information).
4. A master copy of train-the-trainer materials.

I will line up any additional resources I may need—including
administrative support—to provide a quality product that is
computer-compatible with your system.

I estimate that the cost to Edwards & Co. would be in the range of $25,000 to $30,000 including expenses. I would bill you on a monthly basis, as follows:

November 8 ($10,000)
December 8 ($10,000)
December 18 (based on actual time and costs incurred)

As usual, I would provide you with a monthly status report of actual time and expenses so you could track your costs.

Kathleen, once you have made your decisions about priorities and available resources, I would be pleased to provide you with a more detailed proposal geared to the specific needs you have identified. I look forward to continuing to work with you and your associates.

Kindest regards,

Jordan Milgram

- An all-in-one letter with brief proposal is useful in sketching out a project, but always offer to provide a separate proposal with greater details. Because of its length, this letter can be easily faxed.

- Always follow up on a letter proposal in a few days while the subject is still in the mind of the recipient.

Company Name
Address
City, State Zip

Date

Ms. Diana Landry
Chief Financial Officer
Grand Rapids Neighborhood Group
1308 Pontiac Street
Grand Rapids, MI 49505

Dear Diana:

As a long-time admirer of the outstanding work your organization has done in the community, I particularly enjoyed having the opportunity to see how you function from the inside. As you indicated during our meeting, Grand Rapids Neighborhood Group has grown to a point where it needs to dramatically enhance its accounting function so it can continue to serve effectively.

This correspondence outlines the complete scope of work you requested, including objectives, procedures, identification of responsibilities, and estimated fees.

OBJECTIVE

Implement the NDT60 accounting system on Grand Rapids Neighborhood Group's Cortex microcomputer network. Install the NDT60 software, including implementation and setup, training, conversion assistance, and post-conversion support of the Library Master, General Ledger, Accounts Payable and Import Master modules. Provide professional assistance related to this new system and coordinate the bridge to and from the Donor IV and NewGift software. Success of this project is dependent not just on the software, but also on your personnel's skill, effort and willingness to work as a team.

SCOPE OF SERVICES

1. Procedures

   a. Assist in planning implementation of the NDT60 accounting system.
   b. Recommend steps required to successfully install the new system and assist in assembling setup information and accounting data used in the implementation process.
   c. Establish specifications for the bridge from the Donor IV software to capture cash receipt information. (Note: Donor IV software has a "General Ledger Distribution" file that contains information that can be bridged in detail or summary format. The interface (export file) will be written by Donor IV staff.)
   d. Establish specifications for the bridge from the NewGift software to bridge payment schedules for grants issued. (Note: NewGift has a standard bridge but requires minor modification. The interface will be modified by NewGift staff.)
   e. Write the bridge to receive (import) the information into the NDT60 software.

2. Training and Testing

   a. Work with you and your staff during installation and implementation to help you gain a general understanding of the system.
   b. Train in the areas of transaction entry and posting, monthly and year-end reporting procedures, monthly and year-end closing procedures, and periodic back-up procedures.
   c. Upon completion, system test NDT60 to assure it is functioning as intended and is producing accurate financial reports based on your input.

3. Conversion and Post-Conversion Support

   a. Assist in planning and assembling data for the conversion to

NDT60, as required. (Note: Data entry assistance is $30 per hour. This cost is not included in our estimate.)

b. Provide free telephone support for 30 days after conversion. Subsequent charges for support calls are billed in 10 minute units at $12.50 per unit.

Support calls are invoiced weekly. Fees are subject to change annually, effective January 1 of each year, based upon 30-day notice.

YOUR RESPONSIBILITIES

This project demands significant involvement by your accounting personnel. Ultimate success is highly dependent on their effort. To help achieve a smooth and successful implementation, it will be your responsibility to perform the following:

1. Assemble an up-to-date trial balance for all accounts as of the conversion date.

2. Compile a complete list of all vendors/grants payable, including amounts outstanding (by invoice), addresses, phone numbers, vendor terms, vendor classes (if any), and other necessary vendor/grant information. Total amounts outstanding on the vendor listing should agree with total accounts payable from trial balance.

3. Create a complete list of existing endowments with balances as of the conversion date.

4. Include a copy of the financial statements formats desired by the organization for the balance sheet, income statement, and other financial reports.

BENEFITS

When the project is complete, Grand Rapids Neighborhood Group will have successfully converted to the NDT60 integrated accounting system. Benefits include timely, accurate accounting data, ease of data entry, and flexible reporting with a bridge to your gift and donor software.

SOFTWARE COSTS AND PROFESSIONAL FEES

Software costs and fee estimates are summarized on the attached schedule. These fees are effective provided (a) your accounting records are in good order and (b) a staff member can devote full time to the implementation process. Fees will be adjusted to actual accordingly. We will not incur additional hours without written prior approval. Our fee does not include modifications to the NDT60 software.

Our terms are 50% deposit on software costs before we begin. The balance for software costs is due upon installation (actual loading of the software). Our professional fees are billed weekly.

CLOSING

We appreciate the opportunity to service your computer software needs. If you wish to accept this proposal, please sign one copy and return it with a 50% deposit of the software costs.

Sincerely,

Margaret Chase
President

RESPONSE

This letter correctly sets forth the understanding of Grand Rapids Neighborhood Group.

Accepted by	Title	Date

Company Name
Address
City, State Zip

P R O P O S A L

DATE: TO: Diana Landry
SOFTWARE: NDT60   Grand Rapids Neighborhood Group

SOFTWARE COST:
    Library Multi-Record $1,255
      including Report Master
    General Ledger   850
    Accounts Payable   850
    Import Master   645
          TOTAL SOFTWARE: $3,600

PROFESSIONAL FEE ESTIMATE:
                             HOURS
Installation Plan   9
    Identify Responsibilities
    Establish Schedule
    Select Conversion Date

Installation of Software   5
    Install NDT60 Modules on Electra Network
    Set Terminal ID's and Preferences
    Set Printers and Defaults
    Establish Security

Implementation of Modules   9
    Establish Parameter and Master Files
    GL, AP and Custom Financial Statements

Training: All Modules and Backup   9
    Document Procedures
    Demonstrate Hands-On Entry Reporting

Conversion   9
    Define Conversion Tasks and Methods

Build Import from Donor IV and NewGift   18

Coordinate bridge to/from Donor IV and
    NewGift Software   18
    Meet with Grand Rapids Neighborhood
    Group to establish coordination
    specifications. Meet with representatives
    from Donor IV and NewGifts to establish
    responsibilities.

        TOTAL HOURS   77

        TOTAL FEES $6,930

- This departure from the traditional cover letter and separate proposal can be effective when dealing with fairly technical subjects. The letter defines the multitude of issues involved and leads logically into the proposal.

- It is a valuable tool to list the client's responsibilities in the projects; otherwise you may be expected to do more than you think you contracted for.

Company Name
Address
City, State Zip

Date

Ms. Carol Victor
Children's Resources, Inc.
2001 8th Avenue
Neffs, PA 18065

Dear Carol:

I think you'll be pleased with the enclosed proposal because it fulfills two of your key objectives:

1. It gives you the upgrade you need to help you increase your efficiency and services.
2. It's well within the budget parameters you requested.

I wasn't able to address your question about bridging an interface to the high school's mainframe computer, but that's only because my technical staff requires more information before we offer a bid. I'll tell you what we need when we speak about the enclosed numbers.

Thank you for giving me the opportunity to submit a proposal. I'll call you on Tuesday, October 23, to answer any questions and to get the additional information I need.

Sincerely,

Alice Channing

- You can help prepare the reader to think positively simply by stating that you think they will be pleased with your proposal.

- Thank the reader for the opportunity to submit the proposal.

Company Name
Address
City, State Zip

P R O P O S A L

For Carol Victor, Children's Resources, Inc.,
October 10, 19XX

GENERAL:
Children's Resources, Inc. needs to store demographic, teacher &
CST information in databases and be able to quickly and accurately extract information from these relational databases for
various reports. At present, some data is stored in a PlusWorld
4.2 secondary file and accessed through the PlusWorld merge
feature. Other reports are compiled manually.

RECOMMENDATION:
Implement relational databases where the pertinent data can be
stored in individual files. Initially three files (demographic, teacher
& CST) would be established to capture the information.

PlanWorld database software is recommended, since the
Children's Resources staff is familiar with the PlusWorld program.
PlanWorld uses similar keystrokes to execute commands and will
lessen time required for the learning process.

An upgrade to the PlusWorld 5.1 program is also recommended
because it contains many new features that will accommodate and
enhance report printing.

To provide access to the various databases, an Electra multi-user
environment is recommended. An upgrade to a multi-user system
can be done at a later date. This will allow individual users to find
information rapidly, request reports, and print to a spooler so that
all printers may be shared by all users.

THE FOLLOWING COSTS ARE BASED ON USING
CHILDREN'S RESOURCES EXISTING COMPUTER EQUIPMENT

SOFTWARE COSTS:
PlanWorld Educational Pricing $250
    Each additional computer 25

PlusWorld upgrade to 5.1 89
    Each additional computer 25

PlusWorld office upgrade 89
    Each additional computer 25

Note: Serial number or title page from the original
manual is required to qualify for the upgrade price.

TRAINING:

2 Days Training on each program at our Computer Services
Training Classroom. Minimum 4 participants.

Per Participant/per day $125

2 Days Training on each program, on-site at your facility.
Minimum 8 participants.

Per Participant/per day $600

HARDWARE AND ELECTRA PROPOSAL

File Server
1 986 90mhz Clone with 500 meg drive and 8 meg memory,
keyboard, color monitor, 32 bit Lohmann
network board $2,800

1 Electra 7 user PCD network operating system $1,000

2 986 80 mhz LNC Clones with 16 bit Lohmann
network boards, keyboard, color monitor,
4 meg ram $2,500

1 External 500 meg tape backup unit $480

2 Uninterruptible power supply (UGS) 600 Watts $750

Complete installation & setup of network $500

Subtotal $8,030

1 Year Service Contract on all hardware and Elektra Operation
System (workstations, network boards, cabling, server, etc. All
parts and labor 1st year only) $1,300

TOTAL $9,330

• Always label each section clearly. Don't make the reader guess.

• Provide numerical data in tabular form for ease of understanding.

Company Name
Address
City, State Zip

Date

Ms. Barbara Schiff
Office of Training and Education
American Water Filters
Route 8
Millsboro, DE 19966

Dear Barbara:

Thank you for considering THE ACTION GROUP as a training resource for your Professional Excellence Program.

The cost proposal and outline you requested on Interpersonal Communication and Teamwork is enclosed. We've written it to reflect our understanding of your requirements and expectations, and we've included outlines on Presentation Skills and Conflict Resolution, as well.

If you like what you see, we'll be happy to go to the next step and outline our procedures and objectives.

We're excited about the possibility of working with you. I'll call you within a week to get your reaction.

Sincerely,

Bernard Standish

- Remind the client that they requested the information.

- If the prospect hasn't given you as much information as you'd like, give yourself a margin for error by stating that the proposal reflects your understanding of their needs.

PROPOSAL
PROFESSIONAL EXCELLENCE PROGRAM

Phase 1: NEEDS ANALYSIS
- Distribute, collect & score Lande-Torre Type Indicator
- Interview participants

Phase 2: DESIGN/DEVELOPMENT
- Evaluate and modify training objectives based on needs analysis
- Select appropriate modules
- Determine appropriate learning experiences
- Develop content-specific activities
- Design interactive training seminar

Phase 3: DELIVERY OF TRAINING (2 day seminar)
- Co-facilitate
- Use break-out groups
- Model effective training techniques
- Provide opportunities for reflection, practice, and feedback

OUR UNDERSTANDING:
- Contracts will be awarded competitively based on quality, experience, substance, and cost of delivery.
- The Professional Excellence Program will be an integral part of the orientation and training planned for new employees.
- The first series of seminars will be a pilot program.
- Participants in the pilot group will have less than 2 years of service with American Water Filters.

PROCESS:
THE ACTION GROUP will conduct a telephone needs analysis by interviewing all participants in the pilot program. In addition, participants will take the Lande-Torre Type Indicator approximately 3 weeks prior to the training session. The LTTI will be scored at the LT Center for Behavioral Studies.

Based on the information gathered in Phase 1, THE ACTION GROUP will select content-appropriate modules and learning experiences from our Communications modules. Training of the participant group will be facilitated by two of THE ACTION GROUP principals. Subgroups will be used to involve each participant. The needs analysis will also be used to design and modify additional seminars on (1) Conflict Resolution and Negotiation and (2) Designing and Delivering Effective Presentations if either of those contracts should be awarded to THE ACTION GROUP.

Upon completion of the training seminars, THE ACTION GROUP facilitators will be actively involved in the post-seminar critique of the overall design and individual components of the Professional Excellence Program.

BENEFITS:
- THE ACTION GROUP is committed to making the course relevant to your specific needs.
- THE ACTION GROUP principals have combined experience of over 30 years in adult learning.
- THE ACTION GROUP has conducted a similar seminar for the Mid-Level Management Development Program of American Water Filter.
- THE ACTION GROUP facilitators have demonstrated expertise in Program Curriculum Design and Evaluation for many other organizations.
- The ACTION GROUP principals will be a resource for evaluating both the content and process of the Professional Excellence Program. We regularly conduct seminars on Conflict Resolution, Presentation Skills, Written Communication, Interpersonal Communication and Teamwork.

COSTS:

INTERPERSONAL COMMUNICATION & TEAMWORK
Needs Analysis $2,500
Training Delivery 3,800
After Action Critique/Modifications 2,500
TOTAL FOR SERVICES $8,800

Materials: $15 per participant - Minimum $210
Lande-Torre (includes scoring, interpretation)

Travel Expenses (plane, hotel, meals for 2 consultants)

PROGRAM DESIGN SERVICES:
$1,000 per day per consultant

ADDITIONAL TRAINING MODULES:
Effective Presentations (2 days)* $3,000
Plus cost of video tapes/equipment

Conflict Resolution (2 days)* $3,000

* Initial Needs Analysis or After-Action Critique can be expanded
if either of these training modules is awarded, with no additional
costs to the client.

REFERENCES

Ms. Lenore Church
Employee Development Center
Ft. Levering Research Center
Mesa, Washington 99343
(206) 557-4009

Dr. Emily Cramer
Superintendent of Studies
Arlington Center Schools
Arlington, Virginia 22203
(703) 557-4981

Mr. Jerome Wycoff
Director
Neighborhood Centers
1000 Roosevelt Boulevard
Philadelphia, Pennsylvania 19102
(215) 557-1212

Mr. Ethan Winter
Chief, Human Resources
North Dakota Game Commission
Colfax, North Dakota 58018
(701) 557-3377

- Offering additional services (in this case, training modules) at the end of the proposal can generate incremental income.

- Be 100% sure of what your references will say about you (and, of course, that they've given you permission to use them as references in the first place). Sales have been lost because of a presumption of good will.

Preparing Contracts 8

The first thing you'll need to do after getting an assignment is to have the client sign off in writing on the agreed to terms of the project. Since a written proposal usually provides a detailed description of the work you are prepared to do for a client, it can be the basis for a contract. In fact, some clients will simply sign the last page of the proposal as a way of authorizing you to begin your consulting work with them. That's fine, as long as it contains all the items necessary to prove that both the consultant and client have agreed on the essentials. However, a separate contract is the best way to clarify the obligations of both parties.

A contract should also be signed between yourself and any subcontractors doing work for your company. Most of the points that follow apply to both client-consultant and consultant-subcontractor agreements.

There are three options commonly used by companies when they are securing the services of a consultant. These legal documents vary in complexity. As with any legal documents, all contracts should be reviewed by your attorney before you use them in your practice.

A **Letter of Agreement** is the most straightforward and uncomplicated of the three forms of agreement. It is often written by the consultant and calls special attention to the key points of an earlier proposal: the nature and scope of the work to be done; a time schedule for the project; estimated costs including fees and expenses; and any other terms or conditions affecting the project.

A one-page **Agreement Form** can also act as a contract. This type of document usually includes spaces for: services to be provided by the consultant, any special arrangements agreed to, beginning and ending dates, fees and other costs, special payment provisions, and signatures.

A **Contract** is the longest and the most comprehensive of the three legal documents. Contracts deal with a number of issues beyond those in the Letter of

Agreement and Agreement Form. Here are typical subjects covered:

- Scope of the Project—Exactly what tasks and activities will the consultant perform?
- Fees and Payments—How does the consultant calculate fees: on a daily, fixed project fee, monthly retainer? Will a portion be paid in advance? When will remaining payments be made—at scheduled intervals, or upon achievement of specified goals?
- Term of the Contract—What time period will the contract cover?
- Termination—What if things don't work out as planned? How can the contact be ended if either party violates (breeches) the contract's terms? How much notice must be given by either party?
- Independent Contractor—With what language will the consultant's relationship to the client be defined?
- Cancellation Policy—What if the project gets canceled before it begins? What if part of the schedule needs to be adjusted or part of the project needs to be deleted? Will the company pay the consultant for days that have been reserved for this client which cannot easily be "sold" to someone else on short notice?
- Confidentiality—How will the consultant protect himself regarding access to confidential or proprietary information and the client's desire for the consultant not to disclose such information to anyone else?
- Use of Material—What material produced by the consultant will the client be entitled to use? Who will own the material created for the client?
- Assignment of Rights—Can either party assign (transfer) its rights and obligations to another party?
- Arbitration—How will disputes be resolved? Should both parties agree in advance to refer serious disputes to the American Arbitration Association (or a similar organization) for a binding decision?

A Letter of Agreement (8-01), Consulting Agreement (8-02) and Consulting Contract (8-03) are found later in the chapter. Cover letters to accompany the contract (8-04 and 8-05) follow those forms. A Subcontractor's Agreement (8-06) and cover letter (8-07) are shown at the end of the chapter.

Company Name
Address
City, State Zip

Date

Mr. Joseph Wilson
Director of Research Engineering
Larini & Mitchell Chemicals, Inc.
1313 Bayview Road
Richmond, VA 23234

Dear Mr. Wilson:

Thank you for calling yesterday to inform me that my company has been selected as your consultant for the Safety Committee project. As promised, this letter will summarize the key points of our discussion and will serve as an official agreement about the nature of our working relationship.

My role will be to attend several committee meetings in an advisory capacity and to make recommendations directly to you about ways to improve your overall communication systems. Additionally, I will meet with designated committee members to draft, revise and finalize documents being presented to other executive committees. Finally, I will edit any reports being prepared for the president and review them with you prior to final presentation.

I estimate that these activities will take two or three days a month, and we can schedule actual dates at our first planning meeting next week. Using my preferred client rate of $1,000 per day, the cost to you for my consulting services will be between $2,000 and $3,000 per month (plus out-of-pocket expenses for photocopies and telephone calls). I estimate the entire project will take six months. I will send you a monthly report, along with each monthly invoice, so that you can monitor my costs against your budget.

If these terms are acceptable, please sign the attached copy of this letter and return it to me. The other signed copy is for your records.

Please call me if you have any questions. I look forward to working with you on this project.

Sincerely,

Martin Schine
President, S & S Associates

Accepted and agreed to:

_____   _____

Mr. Joseph Wilson   Date
Director of Research Engineering
Larini & Mitchell Chemicals, Inc.

• The simplest contract, a letter of agreement, should contain, at the very least, the following: 1) a description of the services to be provided, 2) fees to be charged, 3) payment schedule, and 4) the duration of the agreement.

• Like any contract, it should be signed by both parties.

Consulting Agreement Form (8-02)

Company Name
Address
City, State Zip

Client's Name: _____

Client's Title: _____

Address: _____
_____
_____

Description of
Services: _____
_____
_____
_____
_____
_____

Beginning Date: _____ Targeted Completion Date: _____

Fees:
    Estimated Fee @$ _____ per day for ___ days : $_____
    Estimated Expenses: $_____

    Total Estimated Costs: $_____

Payment Schedule:
First payment $_____ due upon acceptance of this agreement
Second payment $ _____ due on _____
Third payment $ _____ due on _____

Agreed to: Agreed to:

For _____   For _____
         Client   Consultant

_____   _____
        Signed   Signed

_____   _____
         Date   Date

- This brief agreement form is really a letter of agreement presented in a more structured format.

- For complex, large or long-term projects, a formal contract should be used.

CONSULTING CONTRACT

THIS AGREEMENT MADE THIS _____ DAY OF _____, 19__
BETWEEN _____
(THE "COMPANY") AND _____
(THE "CONSULTANT").

1. The Company hereby retains Consultant, and the Consultant agrees to perform the following services for the Company (collectively the "Services"):

   _____
   _____
   _____

2. In consideration of the performance by Consultant of the Services under this Agreement, the Company agrees to pay Consultant for its time, material, and Services as follows:

   _____
   _____
   _____

   In addition, Consultant shall be entitled to reimbursement for reasonable and substantiated expenses for travel and lodging in the course of performance of its duties.

3. This Agreement covers Services rendered during the period from _____ to _____. This Agreement may be terminated at any time by either party for breach or neglect of duty by the other not remedied within 30 days after written notice by either party. No termination shall prejudice Consultant's rights to payments for Services completed prior to the effective date of termination.

4. All Services shall be performed under this Agreement by Consultant in its capacity as an independent contractor, and not as an agent or employee of the Company. The Consultant shall

supervise the performance of its Services and shall be entitled to control the manner and means by which its Services are to be performed, subject to compliance with this Agreement and any specifications, schedules, or plans approved by the Company.

5. With respect to the initial scheduling of consulting time, Consultant will make every reasonable effort to accommodate Company needs and preferences, subject to existing contractual obligations. In addition, if faced with a cancellation of scheduled time or request for postponement by the Company, Consultant will make every effort to reschedule time so as to minimize potential Company payment responsibility for lost time.

To the extent Consultant for any reason is unable to do so, however, Consultant will bill Company for time scheduled and canceled or postponed, subject to the following terms:

a. Cancellation or postponement occurring within 10 days of scheduled date: 100% of regular fee

b. Cancellation or postponement occurring between 11 and 20 days of scheduled date: 75% of regular fee

c. Cancellation or postponement occurring between 21 and 30 days of scheduled date: 50% of regular fee

d. Cancellation or postponement occurring 31 or more days before scheduled date: No payment

These provisions shall apply irrespective of the cause of the cancellation or postponement.

6. The Consultant acknowledges that in the course of this Agreement it shall have access to confidential and proprietary information of the Company which the Company may make available to the Consultant (the "Confidential Information") and agrees not to disclose or disseminate the Confidential Information without the express prior written consent of the Company.

The term "Confidential Information" shall not include such information as is or becomes part of the public domain through no action or omission of Consultant, which becomes available to Consultant from third parties without knowledge by Consultant of any breach of fiduciary duty, or which the Consultant had in its possession prior to the date of this Agreement.

7. All notices under this Agreement shall be sent by first class mail by overnight courier and/or confirmed telefax to the addresses specified below and any notice sent shall be deemed delivered three days after deliverance in accordance with these terms and conditions:

To Company: To Consultant:

_____   _____
_____   _____
_____   _____
_____   _____

8. All disputes under this Agreement may be arbitrated under the rules of the American Arbitration Association, and any judgments in accordance with the above may be entered in a court of competent jurisdiction.

9. This is the complete agreement and supersedes all prior and contemporaneous understandings relating to the subject matter hereof, may not be amended or modified except in writing, and shall be governed by the laws of the State of _____.

COMPANY

By:_____

CONSULTANT

By:_____

- Any contract you sign should first be shown to your attorney.

- Of course, your attorney should also review any agreement you plan on adopting as your "basic contract."

Company Name
Address
City, State Zip

Date

Mr. John C. Horan
Chief Financial Officer
Tamec Engineering, Inc.
123 Witt Boulevard, Suite 456
Philadelphia, PA 19101

Dear John:

I am looking forward to working with your Regional Vice Presidents on their new strategic business objectives. I have attached a signed copy of the contract.

Thanks again for thinking of me for this assignment. I enjoy working on this type of a project, especially with one of your management teams. Please give me a call if you need any additional information from me before we get started.

Best regards,

Nolan Parks

- An expression of enthusiasm about the project and a simple "thank you for the assignment" when returning a signed contract are appropriate.

Company Name
Address
City, State Zip

Date

Mr. David E. Williams
Senior Vice President
Andrews Pharmaceuticals, Inc.
55 Valley View Parkway
Atlanta, GA 55555

Dear Mr. Williams:

I am pleased to return to you the attached signed contract indicating my intention to begin working on your consulting project. As you know, there were two areas that our attorneys revised or clarified. I appreciate your willingness to define more clearly your "Non-Disclosure" requirements and to include my "Cancellation Clause" for payment of fees when there is an unexpected need for you to revise the schedule.

I am confident that we now have a solid working agreement that will ensure timely and cost-effective results for you on this important project. I am looking forward to working with you during the next six months.

Sincerely,

Marian Andropoulis

- When returning a signed contract that you've revised, point out the areas of change.

- Always thank the client for helping resolve contract issues.

Company Name
Address
City, State Zip

Subcontractor's Name _____

Address

_____

_____

_____

_____

Telephone #   (_____) _____
FAX #   (_____) _____

Project Description

_____

Services to be Provided by Subcontractor

_____

_____

_____

_____

_____

Fee for Services _____

Other Costs

_____

_____

_____

Schedule for Delivery of Services

_____

_____

_____

Payment Schedule

_____

_____

For   _____
                    (Consultant)

        _____   _____
                     Signed   Date

For   _____
                   (Subcontractor)

        _____   _____
                     Signed   Date

• Be sure all services are spelled out, all costs are specified and delivery dates are listed.

Company Name
Address
City, State Zip

William Wiley
33 Midland Ave.
Reno, NV 89509

Dear Bill:

I'm pleased that you'll be able to help with our new assignment from Busby Electronics. I've attached a form outlining what we've agreed your responsibilities and fee will be.

As you know, we've got to get going on this project by the 24th. So if you have any questions or comments, please give me a call as soon as you receive this material. Otherwise, please fax a signed copy to me and then return the original at your convenience.

Kindest regards,

Harvey White

- If you have a tight schedule, let your subcontractor know as soon as possible.

- It's a good idea to have a signed agreement in hand before starting any project. A faxed copy will suffice, but also get the original (which can be sent later) to put in your files.

Credit and Collections 9

The only thing worse than not winning a consulting assignment is winning one and then not getting paid for it. And almost as bad as either of these is to win a job and wait...and wait...and wait for payment.

Most non- and slow-payment problems can be eliminated if a few basic steps are followed:

1. Check the credit status of any company that wants to use your services. Don't be so pleased you've won the job that you ignore this survival procedure.
2. If you're uncertain that a company is creditworthy, send a Request for Credit Information (9-01) and thoroughly check all information provided. Don't assume that because a company official says something is so, it is.
3. Establish a written agreement with your client, stating fee and payment terms.
4. Don't begin work until a company purchase order is issued to you. (Many companies will not pay without an official purchase order, even if a contract has been signed.)
5. Ask for staged payments (e.g., 1/3rd upon agreement, 1/3rd at the midpoint, 1/3rd upon completion), to keep your cash flow healthy.
6. Consider offering a discount for early payment (for example, 1% discount for 10-day payment). Large companies may favor paying early and taking the discount. You'll find it well worth the small amount sacrificed when you see the cash come in quickly.
7. Use clear, readable, professional-looking invoices (9-02 and 9-03).
8. Prepare a series of firm, but courteous collection letters (see 9-04

through 9-07). There's a fine line between demanding what's due you and alienating someone who may give you continued business.

9. Have a professional collection agency assist you with difficult accounts (9-08).

Obtaining Credit Information

If you're fortunate enough to receive work from companies (and government agencies) that are established, recognizable, and reputable, there may not be as great a need to obtain credit data. (Keep in mind, however, that even giant companies have cash crunches.) But it's likely that you'll also generate business from organizations which are not so well-known, and that's where you'll run the greatest risk of being "stung."

One way of obtaining credit information about a prospect is to subscribe to a service such as Dun & Bradstreet—or use their pay-as-you-go service. By calling them (800-544-3867) and paying $75 with your credit card, you can get a report on any company in Dun & Bradstreet's database faxed to you the same day.

You can also do the credit checking on your own by sending the prospect company a Request for Credit Information (9-01). Most accounting departments are used to being asked to provide the requested information. When you receive the names of suppliers, you can ask the suppliers questions regarding the prospect company, such as:

- credit limit provided
- promptness with which payments are made
- frequency of payment disputes, etc.

Some consultants report that the companies from whom they least expect payment delays are often the worst offenders...companies whose names conjure up images of organization, precision, and punctuality. In fact, when times are tough (and they're always tough when it comes to getting paid!) many companies will withhold payment as long as possible.

There are ways to combat slow pay accounts. And the first way is to be certain that the delay isn't of *your* doing. Your own invoice could be the cause.

The Invoice

1. Be sure to send the invoice to the correct address and department. When dealing with large corporations and government agencies, your invoice may need to be sent to an office that's not in the same state, let alone the same building as your client. Always ask how the invoice should be addressed. Don't assume it goes to your contact. An invoice sent to the wrong department or address will, at best, be delayed or, at worst, become misplaced or ignored, causing longer delays and hard feelings.

2. Always reference the purchase order number. In many cases, unless you include the client's authorizing P.O. number on your invoice, you won't be paid.

Although you've completed your work, without a purchase order number your job doesn't exist—as far as the Accounts Payable department is concerned. Don't accept a job without being issued a purchase order first.

3. Include all necessary information on your invoice. Although an invoice can take many forms, you are better off with a simple form that clearly details:

- The client for whom the work was performed
- The correct billing address
- The date the job was issued
- The client's Purchase Order number
- Your invoice date
- Your invoice number
- Your payment terms (e.g., net 30 days, or 2% discount 10 days)
- Description of the service performed
- Total fee (broken down if required by the client)
- Penalty for late payment

It may help expedite payment if you affix a copy of the purchase order to your invoice. Also, be certain how many copies of your invoice are required. For example, submission of a 3-part invoice when a 4-part invoice is required can result in delayed payment. Two styles of invoices (9-02 and 9-03) appear at the end of this chapter. Because of their importance, two additional formats (10-15 and 10-16) appear at the end of Chapter 10.

Preparing Your Own Collection Letters

Consultants awaiting payment sometimes assume that if they are patient, they'll be paid. But sometimes:

- The client contact is not aware the accounting department has held up payment. By being reminded, they can help expedite a check.
- Your invoice may never have arrived (rare, but it happens!).
- Your invoice may have been misplaced, and the reminder gets the process rolling again.

The point is, you can't afford to remain silent. Clients expect to pay you, but they occasionally need a helpful reminder or two.

Many consultants feel that the best way to get paid is to deal directly with the individual with whom they contracted. Sending letters to a faceless accounting department is often nonproductive; accounting people do not set policy, they follow it. Intercession by your contact can cut through an otherwise impenetrable defense.

When seeking payment, remember that everything you write to a client is a reflection of you and your company. Even though money may be owed you, there is a right way and a wrong way to ask for it. Although a very harsh, "take no prisoners," approach may be successful in putting a check in your hands quickly, it may also be the last time you get work from that client—or anyone they decide to tell about your "attitude."

The best way to approach writing a collection letter to your contact is to think of it as a sales letter. You are trying to persuade someone to do something. An effective letter of persuasion concentrates on the reader, making it clear to him or her why the requested action is of value. Letters that are written solely from your perspective ("I earned that money, and I want it now...") are often perceived as being negative and "whiny." That doesn't mean you can't or shouldn't ask for what is rightfully yours. It simply means you don't want to create an adversary.

A good collection letter should talk about:

- the value of your work
- any savings to the company
- your expectation to be paid for a job well done

Collection letters 9-04 and 9-05 take a firm tone, but they never cross the line into rudeness or unprofessionalism. Even the final letter in this series (9-06), which threatens to turn the account over to a collection agency, offers an olive branch and requests cooperation. One thing to remember is never to threaten unless you're prepared to back it up.

If your contact tells you that they are unable to do anything, and that you must write to the Accounts Payable supervisor, remember that this accounting person does not know you or the circumstances of the job. When you're writing to someone who is unfamiliar with your situtation, get to the point quickly and summarize the key information the recipient needs to know. It will be helpful to highlight the following information, before you get to the body of the letter:

Client's Purchase Order number and date
Description/title of work performed
Amount past due

Your invoice number and date
Number of days overdue

The letter should be courteous, but firm. As one consultant puts it, "Be brief, not abrupt." A helpful, pleasant tone will often gain you allies; a nasty, sarcastic, threatening tone may be taken as a challenge. You don't want to make enemies; you just want to get paid.

The Letter about Outstanding Invoice, to Accounting Department (9-07) is an example of this kind of letter. It is found later in the chapter.

Hiring a Collection Agency

No matter how well you've written your collection letters and cultivated your contact, you may be unable to collect the dollars due you. When that happens, you have two primary options:

1. Forget about it, and learn from the experience.
2. Hire a collection agency.

Many consultants dislike using collection agencies because they're afraid of alienating the client. Of course, given that the client isn't paying your invoices, there probably isn't much to lose.

Once you decide that you need the services of a collection agency, use the letter at the end of this chapter (9-08) to ensure that the company is legitimate.

Company Name
Address
City, State Zip

Date

Ms. Elaine Malesta
Fox Haven Nursing Homes
983 W. Maiden Lane
Wilmington, DE 19888

Dear Ms. Malesta:

We've been asked to perform consulting services for your organization. Prior to extending credit for those services, we need the following questions answered. If you'll take a moment to complete this form, we can begin our work on your organization's behalf. ALL RESPONSES WILL BE HELD IN STRICTEST CONFIDENCE.

Thank you for your speedy attention.

Sincerely,

Thomas Worth

1. How many years have you been in business? _____

2. Are the name and address shown above correct? __Yes __No. If not, please make all necessary changes above.

3. Please list your bank account number:

_____

4. What is the name, address, and phone number of your bank?
Name _____
Address _____
_____
Phone # (   ) _____

5. Please list the addresses, phone numbers and contact names of three vendors you use on a regular basis:
Name _____
Address _____
_____
Contact _____ Phone # (   )_____

Name _____
Address _____
_____
Contact _____ Phone # (   )_____

Name _____
Address _____
_____
Contact _____ Phone # (   )_____

6. What is your payment policy? ____ 30 ____ 60 ____ 90 days

Please mail this form to the address shown above, or fax it to 302-555-1882.

Thank you.

- A company unwilling to provide such information is probably not a company for whom you wish to work.

- This form is only the first step in checking the credit worthiness of a prospective client. The second, and critical step, is calling the vendors and bank.

Invoice, Horizontal Format (9-02)

Company Name
Address
City, State Zip

INVOICE TO:

Mr. Howard Warfield
Purchasing Agent
Powers Construction Corp.
19 West Oldfield Boulevard
Dallas, TX 75371

DATE OF ORDER:	PURCHASE ORDER NUMBER:	INVOICE DATE:	INVOICE TERMS:	INVOICE NUMBER:
06/22/XX	11KAL33872	8/11/XX	Net 30 Days	NR1448

DESCRIPTION OF SERVICE	UNIT PRICE	AMOUNT
Reorganization of Procedures Manuals for Accounting and Warehousing	$900.00 ea.	$1,800.00
	TOTAL DUE	$1,800.00

Late Charges: 1-1/2% interest will be added monthly to late payments. Please be prompt to avoid late charges.

THANK YOU

- Pertinent data can be included on one line.

- Imprint your penalty charges on the invoice. It's a reminder that may force some accounts into paying on time.

Company Name
Address
City, State Zip

I N V O I C E

Date: 10/22/XX

Ms. Wilma Bowman
Carlin & White, Inc.
Crown Oak Centre/Suite 330
Orlando, FL 32818.   Invoice No. 00375

Customer Purchase Order: A302-00-13KL (Issued 5/12/XX)
Terms: On Receipt

SERVICE PROVIDED   PRICE

Report on feasibility of development
of fashion ski wear line, and analysis and
projection of marketing success $6,000.00

                        LESS Initial Payment   - $2,000.00

                            TOTAL DUE $4,000.00

T H A N K   Y O U

Late Charges: 1-1/2% interest will be added monthly to late
payments. Please be prompt and avoid late charges.

- Don't make the customer guess what they are receiving. Clearly label your invoices.

- If partial payment has been made, show it. It will help speed the payment process to indicate all financial transactions that have been connected with the job.

Company Name
Address
City, State Zip

Date

Mr. Leopold Weston
Coronet Business Systems
3400 W. Saginaw Street
Anchorage, AK 99511

Dear Mr. Weston:

It hardly seems like 60 days have passed since we completed our review and analysis of your fleet needs. By this time you've probably had the opportunity to implement some of our recommendations, and you should be well on your way to saving tens of thousands of dollars this year alone.

Since we had agreed that the final $4,000 payment for the report would be issued upon completion and presentation, I'd appreciate it if you'd give your accounting department a gentle nudge, particularly since they'll be the beneficiary of all the extra money we've found for them!

It was great working with you. I hope we can be of service again soon.

Cordially,

Hal Burton

- Remind the client of how satisfactory your service was. Keep the tone of the letter positive.

- Never blame your client for the payment problem. It's likely not their fault, and saying so will only make them defensive.

Company Name
Address
City, State Zip

Date

Mr. Leopold Weston
Coronet Business Systems
3400 W. Saginaw Street
Anchorage, AK 99511

Dear Mr. Weston:

It's disappointing to perform a service—particularly one that has been as well received as our review and analysis of your fleet needs—and then have to repeatedly ask for payment.

One thing we discovered in our overview of your business is that you have a well-deserved reputation for dependability and on-time service. It's hard to believe that your Accounts Payable department doesn't extend the same courtesy to your suppliers that you do to your clients.

Will you please take whatever steps are necessary to expedite the final payment? Thanks for your help.

Sincerely,

Hal Burton

- Mention the client's excellent reputation. It may strike a responsive chord.

- Express disappointment that you've fulfilled your end of the transaction and they haven't.

Company Name
Address
City, State Zip

Date

Mr. Leopold Weston
Coronet Business Systems
3400 W. Saginaw Street
Anchorage, AK 99511

Dear Mr. Weston:

We're frustrated that, 120 days after completion of our fleet analysis review, we still haven't been paid. Adding to the frustration is our inability to get any answers as to why payment has been delayed for so long.

Since all communication is one-way, we have no choice but to take whatever action is necessary to be paid for our work. If we don't receive our $4,000 payment within 10 days of the date of this letter, we'll be forced to turn this matter over to a collection agency.

Will you please let us hear from you before we take additional steps? We're certain this can be resolved, but we can't do it without your help.

Sincerely,

Hal Burton

- Even at this late date, invite dialogue. You may be surprised to receive an offer for payment.

- If you make a threat, follow through with it if your conditions aren't met. You will receive no respect for being a doormat.

Company Name
Address
City, State Zip

Date

Mr. Martin Chasen
Accounts Payable
Coronet Business Systems
3400 W. Saginaw Street
Anchorage, AK 99511

Re: PO# 23441-31
Invoice # 9931 Dated July 9, 19xx
$4,000 payment—90 days overdue

Dear Mr. Chasen:

Leopold Weston suggested I contact you concerning the outstanding invoice indicated above. I've attached copies of both the purchase order and invoice.

Our work was completed on time as called for in our contract, and Mr. Weston has stated that he approved payment of our invoice. I am particularly concerned since payment is now 90 days late.

I would appreciate your checking into this matter. I'll call you on the 20th to check on payment status. In the meanwhile, if you need anything from me, please call or fax me.

Thank you for your cooperation in this matter.

Sincerely,

Hal Burton

cc: Leopold Weston

- Include all the information the accounting department will need to pursue the payment, including copies of both the purchase order and invoice.

- Stating when you'll call should help ensure that your inquiry will be pursued. Of course, be sure to call on the stated date.

Company Name
Address
City, State Zip

Date

Mr. Charles Liebrandt
Interstate Collections, Inc.
255 W. Magnolia Avenue
Ann Arbor, MI 48109

Dear Mr. Liebrandt:

I'm considering using a collection agency to help with seriously past due business accounts. If you'd like to be considered, please complete the following questions and return the attached form to me (to speed up the process, you can fax it to me at 313-555-0890). I'll call you for a face-to-face meeting after I have the chance to review the information.

Thanks for your time. I hope we have the chance to work together.

Sincerely,

Allen Solowicz

Company Name
Address
City, State Zip

1. How many years have you been in the collection business? _____

2. Is your company licensed in Michigan? _____Yes _____No
   License # _____

3. Is your company bonded in Michigan? _____Yes _____No
   Bonding # _____

4. What is your fee structure?
   _____
   _____

5. How many contacts will you make per account? _____

6. Please provide three accounts, including contact names and phone
   numbers, who I may call for a reference:
   Name _____
   Address _____
   _____
   Contact _____ Phone # (   )_____

   Name _____
   Address _____
   _____
   Contact _____ Phone # (   )_____

   Name _____
   Address _____
   _____
   Contact _____ Phone # (   )_____

- Be sure you know who is representing you. Don't be afraid to ask questions.

- Do not accept a collection agency's services without checking references.

Record Keeping Forms 10

Every business, and consulting is no exception, needs a variety of record keeping forms if it is to run effectively and efficiently. For example, you will want to create records about prospects and clients, found in forms 10-01 through 10-04. You should also maintain information about subcontractors (10-05 and 10-06), and phone calls made and received (10-07 and 10-08).

Other forms included in this chapter are designed to expedite routine financial transactions. There are purchase order forms (10-09 and 10-10) and forms for recording expenses (10-11 and 10-12), plus a form for calculating per diem costs (10-13). A Job Cost Estimating Worksheet (10-14) is also located in this chapter. Two invoice forms for billing clients are provided (10-15 and 10-16) as is an Invoice Ledger Form (10-17) for keeping track of outstanding invoices. The Cash Flow Estimate Form (10-18) and Monthly Business Expense Form (10-19) are designed to budget and control expenses.

One of the most important aspects of marketing your services is to continually evaluate your promotional and advertising programs. Several forms are provided to do this (10-20 through 10-22). The Annual Marketing Plan form (10-23) will help you structure your marketing activities throughout the year. Also provided are an Insertion Order for Advertising Space (10-24) and a List Rental Purchase Order (10-25) to buy advertising space and rent mailing lists.

Since time is your most valuable asset, you will want to take a close look at how you are spending your time. Forms 10-26 through 10-28 will aid you in that important task.

PROSPECT PROFILE

Contact Name _____

Title _____

Company _____

Address

_____

_____

_____

_____

Telephone # (_____)_____

FAX #   (_____)_____

Referred By _____

Type of Business _____

Age of Business _____

Sales Territory _____

Number of Employees _____

Public Company? (Yes/No) _____

Est. Annual Sales _____

Description of Company's Products/Services

_____

_____

_____

_____

_____

_____

Company's Competitors

_____

_____

Has the company used consultants before?_____

For what kinds of projects?

_____

_____

_____

_____

Were they satisified with the consultants they used? If not, why not?

_____

_____

_____

_____

Other Comments

_____

_____

_____

_____

_____

_____

_____

_____

_____

_____

- Gather as much information about your prospect as you can during your initial conversation—and through research you do before the first call.

PROSPECT RECORD

Contact Name _____

Title _____

Company _____

Address

_____

_____

_____

_____

Telephone # (_____)_____

FAX #   (_____)_____

CONTACT HISTORY

Type of contact (phone/meeting)	Date	Results	Next Follow-up
_____	_____	_____	_____
_____	_____	_____	_____
_____	_____	_____	_____
_____	_____	_____	_____
_____	_____	_____	_____
_____	_____	_____	_____
_____	_____	_____	_____
_____	_____	_____	_____
_____	_____	_____	_____
_____	_____	_____	_____
_____	_____	_____	_____
_____	_____	_____	_____
_____	_____	_____	_____

• By keeping careful records of your prospect contacts, you'll increase the chances of converting prospects to clients.

CLIENT PROFILE

Contact Name _____

Title _____

Company _____

Address

_____

_____

_____

_____

Telephone # (_____)_____

FAX #   (_____)_____

Type of Business _____

Age of Business _____

Sales Territory _____

Number of Employees _____

Public Company? (Yes/No) _____

Annual Sales _____

Federal ID#/SS# _____

Billing Contact Name _____

Billing Contact Title _____

Billing Address

_____

_____

_____

_____

Preferred Billing Terms _____

Send how many copies of invoice _____

PERSONAL INFORMATION
Spouse's Name _____

Children's Names and Ages
_____
_____

Hobbies/Interests
_____
_____

Other Information
_____
_____
_____

Comments
_____
_____
_____
_____
_____
_____
_____
_____

• Maintain complete information about your client contacts as well as information about the companies for whom they work.

CLIENT RECORD

Contact Name _____

Title _____

Company _____

Address

_____

_____

_____

_____

Telephone # (_____)_____

FAX # (_____)_____

Referred By _____

Date of First Contact _____

PROJECT HISTORY

Description	Date Completed	Fee
_____	_____	_____
_____	_____	_____
_____	_____	_____
_____	_____	_____
_____	_____	_____
_____	_____	_____
_____	_____	_____
_____	_____	_____
_____	_____	_____

REFERRALS REQUESTED

Purpose	Date Referral Requested	Date Referral Sent	Outcome
_____	_____	_____	_____
_____	_____	_____	_____
_____	_____	_____	_____
_____	_____	_____	_____
_____	_____	_____	_____
_____	_____	_____	_____

• This form allows you to maintain an up-to-date listing of projects you have done and are doing for your clients. It's also helpful when requesting referrals.

SUBCONTRACTOR PROFILE

Contact Name _____

Title _____

Company _____

Address

_____

_____

_____

_____

Telephone # (_____)_____

FAX #   (_____)_____

Federal ID#/SS# _____

Nature of Services Offered

_____

_____

_____

_____

_____

Fee $_____ per day

Other charges

_____

_____

_____

_____

_____

Recommended by

_____

_____

Comments

_____

_____

_____

_____

_____

_____

_____

_____

_____

_____

_____

_____

_____

_____

- Maintain records of all subcontractors whom you might want to use. Of particular importance to note is their specialty and their fee.

SUBCONTRACTOR RECORD

Contact Name _____

Title _____

Company _____

Address

_____

_____

_____

_____

Telephone # (_____)_____

FAX #   (_____)_____

Project	Date Assigned	Date Completed	Cost	Comments
_____	_____	_____	_____	_____
				_____
				_____
_____	_____	_____	_____	_____
				_____
				_____
_____	_____	_____	_____	_____
				_____
				_____
_____	_____	_____	_____	_____
				_____
				_____
_____	_____	_____	_____	_____
				_____
				_____
_____	_____	_____	_____	_____
				_____

- Recording subcontractor assignments provides a good way of evaluating their performance.

- Indicate any problems in the Comments section.

DAILY TELEPHONE LOG

Date _____

Contact	Time	Summary Of Discussion

- One of the most valuable records a consultant can have is a telephone log with notes about conversations. You'll be surprised to find how often you'll refer to this form.

- Keep your logs for at least one year, and preferably longer.

TELEPHONE CONTACT LOG

Date _____

Name_____

Title _____

Company _____

___ Client _____ Prospect _____ Other (specify)_____

Purpose of call
_____
_____

Results ___ Schedule meeting ___ Send literature
        ___ Send proposal
        ___ Other (specify) _____

Next follow up date _____

Comments
_____
_____
_____
_____
_____
_____
_____
_____
_____
_____

- Every follow-up call should be put in writing to be sure that your records are complete, and that you have a systematic way of pursuing new assignments.

- Always follow up. Don't assume the person will get back to you.

Company Name
Address
City, State Zip

PURCHASE ORDER

Purchase Order # _____
(Show this number on all correspondence)

Date _____

Terms _____

Date Required _____

To:
_____
_____
_____
_____

Ship Via _____

Ship To :
_____
_____
_____
_____

Description	Qty.	Item #	Unit Price	Total
_____	_____	_____	_____	_____
_____	_____	_____	_____	_____
_____	_____	_____	_____	_____
_____	_____		Grand Total	_____

Please submit 3 copies of your invoice.

Authorized by _____ Date _____

- Every purchase order should have a number. Use this number on all correspondence relating to the order and ask your suppliers to do so as well.

- Verbal purchase orders should be followed up in writing to avoid later disputes.

Purchase Order for Services (10-10)

Company Name
Address
City, State Zip

PURCHASE ORDER

Purchase Order # _____
(Show this number on all correspondence)

Date _____

Terms _____

Date Required _____

To:

_____
_____
_____
_____

Description of Services

_____
_____
_____
_____
_____
_____
_____
_____

Total for services _____

Please submit 3 copies of your invoice.

Authorized by _____ Date _____

• Include a full description of the services.

• Sign all purchase orders and keep a photocopy. Unsigned orders provide far less control since anyone could prepare one bearing your company's name.

Billable Office Expenses (10-11)

BILLABLE OFFICE EXPENSES

Client _____

For Month of _____, 19__

TELEPHONE/FAX

Date	(P)hone or (F)ax	Phone # Called	Purpose	Amount
_____	_____	_____	_____	_____
_____	_____	_____	_____	_____
_____	_____	_____	_____	_____
_____	_____	_____	_____	_____
_____	_____	_____	_____	_____
_____	_____	_____		_____
			Subtotal	_____

POSTAGE/SHIPPING

Date	Description	Amount
_____	_____	_____
_____	_____	_____
_____	_____	_____
_____	_____	_____
_____	_____	_____
	Subtotal	_____

PRINTING/PHOTOCOPYING

Date	Description	Amount
_____	_____	_____
_____	_____	_____
_____	_____	_____
_____	_____	_____
_____	_____	_____
	Subtotal	_____

OTHER EXPENSES

Date	Description	Amount
	Subtotal	
	TOTAL	

- Don't overlook the importance of keeping accurate records for billing direct expenses to clients.

- At the end of the month—or the end of the project (depending on what your contract calls for)—simply pull out these forms and prepare your invoices.

BILLABLE TRAVEL EXPENSES

Client _____

For Month of _____, 19__

AIR/TRAIN FARE

Date	Description	Amount
_____	_____	_____
_____	_____	_____
_____	_____	_____
_____	_____	_____
_____	_____	_____

Subtotal _____

GROUND TRANSPORTATION
(Rental car/taxis/parking/tolls)

Date	Description	Amount
_____	_____	_____
_____	_____	_____
_____	_____	_____
_____	_____	_____
_____	_____	_____

Subtotal _____

OTHER EXPENSES

Date	Description	Amount
____	_____	____
____	_____	____
____	_____	____
____	_____	____
____	_____	____
____	_____	____

Subtotal _____

TOTAL _____

- Record travel expenses as soon as they are incurred to avoid the nightmare of having to go back over months of records to reconstruct expenses.

- Keep receipts for all charges for at least three years.

PER DIEM CALCULATION WORKSHEET

Hotel room   _____

Breakfast   _____

Lunch   _____

Dinner   _____

Car rental   _____

Taxis   _____

Other _____   _____

Other _____   _____

Total Per Diem Cost   _____

- Many clients prefer to be billed for travel expenses on a per diem basis, rather than for actual expenses incurred. This form helps you calculate per diem expenses.

- Of course, per diem expenses for each trip must be calculated individually so that accurate costs are used.

JOB COST ESTIMATING WORKSHEET

LABOR	# of days	x	daily rate (includes markup for profit)	=
Consultant	_____		_____	_____
Subcontractor(s)	_____		_____	_____
Administrative	_____		_____	_____
Other _____	_____		_____	_____
			Sub Total	_____

TRAVEL EXPENSES

Airline	_____		_____	_____
Car rental	_____		_____	_____
Hotel	_____		_____	_____
Meals	_____		_____	_____
Misc.	_____		_____	_____
			Sub Total	_____

SUPPLIES/PHONE

Printing	_____
Postage	_____
Phone calls/Faxes	_____
Other _____	_____
Other _____	_____
Sub Total	_____
TOTAL	_____

- Knowing what the project will cost is essential for both you and your client. Estimate as accurately as you can.

- This critical step must, of course, be completed before the proposal stage, and depends largely on the interview with your prospect.

Company Name
Address
City, State Zip

INVOICE

Date _____   Client PO # _____

Invoice # _____   Terms _____

To:
_____
_____
_____
_____

SERVICES

Description   Amount
_____   _____
_____   _____
_____   _____
_____   _____
                      Sub total   _____

OUT-OF-POCKET EXPENSES

Description   Amount
_____   _____
_____   _____
_____   _____
_____   _____
                      Sub total   _____

Total Due for Payment on or before June 1, 19xx   _____

• This invoice breaks out each item. Some clients prefer this method of billing.

Invoice for Services, Non-Detailed Charges (10-16)

Company Name
Address
City, State Zip

INVOICE

Date _____

Invoice # _____

Client PO # _____

Terms _____

To:

_____
_____
_____
_____

Services

_____
_____
_____
_____
_____
_____

Sub total   _____

Expenses

_____
_____

Sub total   _____

Total Due for Payment on or before June 1, 19xx _____

- One way to help ensure timely payments is to indicate the date payment is due next to the total.

INVOICE LEDGER

Month/Year _____

Invoice #	Client	Invoice Date	Date Due	Total
_____	_____	_____	_____	_____
_____	_____	_____	_____	_____
_____	_____	_____	_____	_____
_____	_____	_____	_____	_____
_____	_____	_____	_____	_____
_____	_____	_____	_____	_____
_____	_____	_____	_____	_____
_____	_____	_____	_____	_____
_____	_____	_____	_____	_____
_____	_____	_____	_____	_____
_____	_____	_____	_____	_____
_____	_____	_____	_____	_____
_____	_____	_____	_____	_____
_____	_____	_____	_____	_____
_____	_____	_____	_____	_____
_____	_____	_____	_____	_____
_____	_____	_____	_____	_____
_____	_____	_____	_____	_____
_____	_____	_____	_____	_____
_____	_____	_____	_____	_____
_____	_____	_____	_____	_____
_____	_____	_____	_____	_____
_____	_____	_____	_____	_____

Grand Total _____

- Knowing how large your outstanding invoices are, and whether any are overdue, is one of the major steps to avoiding serious cash flow problems.

- Update this report monthly and you'll always know the status of your receivables.

Cash Flow Estimate Form (10-18)

ESTIMATED CASH FLOW FOR 19___

	Jan	Feb	Mar	Apr	May	Jun	Jul	Aug	Sep	Oct	Nov	Dec
CASH INCOME												
Fees												
Other _____												
Total income												
CASH EXPENSES												
Rent												
Utilities												
Telephone												
Auto												
Payroll												
Marketing												
Administration												
Office supplies												
Professional												
Insurance												
Travel												
Taxes												
Other _____												
Other _____												
Other _____												
Ending cash												

- The cash flow form is probably the most important tool during the early years of a consulting business, when cash is dearest. But it will always play an important role, since any successful company needs to keep a vigilant eye on the money going in and out of the business.

MONTHLY EXPENSES

Month/Year_____

	Budget	Actual
Office		
- Rent	$ _____	$ _____
- Utilities	$ _____	$ _____
- Telephone	$ _____	$ _____
- Photocopying	$ _____	$ _____
- Postage	$ _____	$ _____
- Repairs & Maintenance	$ _____	$ _____
- Equipment & Furniture	$ _____	$ _____
- Materials & Supplies	$ _____	$ _____
- Payroll	$ _____	$ _____
Automobile		
- Lease	$ _____	$ _____
- Gas & oil	$ _____	$ _____
- Repairs	$ _____	$ _____
- Parking/Tolls	$ _____	$ _____
Insurance		
- Medical	$ _____	$ _____
- Disability	$ _____	$ _____
- Automobile	$ _____	$ _____
- Office	$ _____	$ _____
Travel-Related Expenses		
- Airfare	$ _____	$ _____
- Hotel	$ _____	$ _____
- Meals	$ _____	$ _____
- Car Rental	$ _____	$ _____
- Miscellaneous	$ _____	$ _____

Marketing $ _____ $ _____

Entertainment $ _____ $ _____

Subcontractor Fees $ _____ $ _____

Professional Development
- Books/Journals $ _____ $ _____
- Association Fees $ _____ $ _____

Professional Services
- Accounting $ _____ $ _____
- Legal $ _____ $ _____

Taxes $ _____ $ _____

         TOTAL $ _____ $ _____

- Budget your expenses each month and then record the actual amount. Adjust your budget in subsequent months if you notice that actual expenses aren't in line with budgeted items.

TELEMARKETING COLD CALL EVALUATION FORM

CALLING PERIOD
From _____ To _____

Number of calls placed _____
Number of interviews resulting from calls _____
Percentage of interviews to calls _____
Number of assignments resulting from calls _____
Dollar value of assignments resulting from calls _____

Source of phone numbers
_____
_____

____ Script attached

Description of script used
_____
_____
_____

____ Follow-up materials attached

Description of follow-up materials
_____
_____
_____

First time script was used? ____ Yes ____ No

Problems encountered with script
_____
_____

Suggested changes to improve script
_____
_____

- Track all your cold calling, both to evaluate it and to increase its effectiveness.

- Follow-up materials are just as important as the telemarketing script itself. Be sure to fine tune both as you get feedback from your initial efforts.

ADVERTISING EVALUATION FORM

Type (check one)

_____ Newspaper ad
_____ Magazine ad

Publication name   _____

Issue date   _____

Circulation   _____

_____ Ad Attached

Description of ad

_____
_____
_____

Key # (i.e. Dept. #) _____

First time ad was used? _____ Yes _____ No

Cost of ad   _____
Cost of ad preparation   _____

TOTAL COST OF AD   _____

Number of inquiries from ad   _____

Number of interviews resulting from ad   _____

Number of assignments resulting from ad   _____

Dollar value of assignments resulting from ad   _____

- Each ad you run should be logged and followed through so that you can determine if it was effective.

- Keep in mind that advertising can produce results over a year or more, depending on the medium used (i.e. daily newspaper ads produce the fastest response; monthly magazines can produce responses for two years or longer).

DIRECT MAIL EVALUATION FORM

Mail date _____

List Description	Key #	Quantity Mailed	# of Inquiries	# of Interviews	# of Assign-ments	$ Value of Assign-ments
_____	____	_____	_____	_____	_____	_____
_____	____	_____	_____	_____	_____	_____
_____	____	_____	_____	_____	_____	_____
_____	____	_____	_____	_____	_____	_____
_____	____	_____	_____	_____	_____	_____
_____	____	_____	_____	_____	_____	_____
_____	____	_____	_____	_____	_____	_____
_____	____	_____	_____	_____	_____	_____

____ Direct mail piece attached

Description of direct mail piece

_____

_____

_____

First time mailing piece was used? _____ Yes _____ No

Cost of printing and mailing per thousand pieces _____

Cost of preparing direct mail piece _____

Total cost of mailing _____

• Any time you prepare a mailing, be sure to place an identifying number (key number) on the reply device so you can trace responses to the lists that generated them.

• As with magazine and newspaper ads, keep careful track of your direct mail efforts so that you can evaluate whether they are producing the desired results.

Annual Marketing Plan (10-23)

ANNUAL MARKETING PLAN FOR 19__

	Promotional Activity	Objective	Cost
January			
February			
March			
April			
May			
June			

	Promotional Activity	Objective	Cost
July	_____	_____	_____
	_____	_____	_____
	_____	_____	_____
	_____	_____	_____
August	_____	_____	_____
	_____	_____	_____
	_____	_____	_____
	_____	_____	_____
September	_____	_____	_____
	_____	_____	_____
	_____	_____	_____
	_____	_____	_____
October	_____	_____	_____
	_____	_____	_____
	_____	_____	_____
	_____	_____	_____
November	_____	_____	_____
	_____	_____	_____
	_____	_____	_____
	_____	_____	_____
December	_____	_____	_____
	_____	_____	_____
	_____	_____	_____
	_____	_____	_____
		TOTAL $	_____

- Even if your marketing schedule is a light one, it's important to plan it on an annual basis so that you can be confident your objectives are covered—and that you don't exceed your budget.

Insertion Order for Advertising Space (10-24)

Company Name
Address
City, State Zip

INSERTION ORDER FOR ADVERTISING SPACE

Date _____

Purchase Order # _____
(Show this number on all correspondence)

Terms _____

To:

_____
_____
_____
_____

Enclosed is _____ Artwork _____ Film

For our advertisement scheduled to appear in:

Publication _____

Issue date(s) _____

_____ 4-color ad _____ 2-color ad _____black & white ad

Ad size _____

Ad cost _____

Special instructions
_____
_____

Authorized by _____ Date _____

- An insertion order is a combination of a contract and instruction sheet to a publication regarding your ad. Therefore, it's important that the form be filled out carefully and completely.

Company Name
Address
City, State Zip

LIST RENTAL PURCHASE ORDER

Date _____

Purchase Order # _____
(Show this number on all correspondence)

Terms _____

To:
_____
_____
_____
_____

List required no later than _____

Ship to:
_____
_____
_____
_____

Provide names on _____ labels _____ magnetic tape

      If on labels, provide them _____ 4-up _____ 1-up
      _____ Other (specify) _____

      _____ Cheshire labels _____ Pressure sensitive labels

      If on mag tape, provide in the following
      format _____

List description	Quantity	Key #	Cost/ thousand	Total cost
			TOTAL	

Special instructions

Authorized by _____ Date _____

• This form is used for ordering mailing lists. Your list broker will submit a similar form to the list owners. However, it's a good idea for you to put your order to the list broker in writing, as well, to avoid misunderstandings.

DAILY TIME LOG

Date _____

	Activity	Comments	If billable, specify client	Code
7:00				
7:30				
8:00				
8:30				
9:00				
9:30				
10:00				
10:30				
11:00				
11:30				
Noon				
12:30				
1:00				
1:30				
2:00				
2:30				
3:00				
3:30				
4:00				
4:30				
5:00				
5:30				
6:00				
6:30				
7:00				

- Your most valuable resource is time. Guard it jealously and use it effectively. A time log, in addition to being a necessity for client billing, provides the means for evaluating how your time is spent.

- Code each activity as Administrative (A), Consulting (C), Marketing (M), Personal (P), or Other (O) so that you can analyze the use of your time.

Time Analysis Worksheet (10-27)

HOW DO YOU MANAGE YOUR TIME?

Based on information supplied on your time sheets, analyze the amount of time you are spending on specific activities each week:

Activity	Hours Spent	Percentage of Time Spent	Too Much	Too Little	Just Right
Marketing	_____	_____	_____	_____	_____
Administration	_____	_____	_____	_____	_____
Consulting	_____	_____	_____	_____	_____
Personal	_____	_____	_____	_____	_____
Other	_____	_____	_____	_____	_____

2. In the beginning, most consultants will need to spend the greatest proportion of their time marketing their practice.

   Does your analysis show that you are spending sufficient time in marketing-related activities? _____ Yes _____ No
   (Keep in mind that your priorities will change as your consulting business grows.)

3. Are you spending too much time on office administration? ___ Yes ___ No

4. What changes (if any) will you make to use your time more wisely?

   _____
   _____
   _____
   _____

• Maximize the time you have by analyzing how it is used. Change your time allocations if you see that you are not accomplishing your goals.

TIME MANAGEMENT WORKSHEET

Week of _____

INCOME SUMMARY

Total Fees $ _____

Other Income $ _____

TOTAL INCOME $ _____

ACTIVITY SUMMARY

\# Available work days   _____

\# Days charged to clients   _____

\# Days developing new business   _____

\# Days administrative duties   _____

\# Days other activities   _____

ANALYSIS

Need to increase revenue by $ _____

Need to increase billable time by   _____ days

Need to increase marketing time by   _____ days

Need to decrease administrative time by   _____ days

- There are several ways to increase your income, in addition to raising your fee, all of which involve adjusting the amount of time you spend on various activities.

- Review the use of your time every three months in the first year of your practice, every six months in the second year, and annually thereafter.

Index by Title

Index by Subject

R

Record keeping, 253
 cash flow, **(10-18), 277**
 client information sheets, **(10-03),**
  257-258; (10-04), 259-260
 expenses, billable office, **(10-11),**
  268-269
 expenses, billable travel, **(10-12),**
  270-271
 expenses, monthly, **(10-19), 278-279**
 invoice ledger, **(10-17), 276**
 invoices, **(9-02), 244; (9-03), 245;**
  (10-15), 274; (10-16), 275
 job cost estimating worksheet,
  (10-14), 273
 marketing evaluation forms
  advertising, **(10-21), 281**
  direct mail, **(10-22), 282**
  telemarketing, **(10-20), 280**
 marketing plan, **(10-23), 283-284**
 per diem expenses worksheet,
  (10-13), 272
 prospect information sheets, **(10-01),**
  254-255; (10-02), 256
 purchase orders
  for advertising space, **(10-24),**
   285
  for goods, **(10-09), 266**
  for mailing list rental, **(10-25),**
   286-287
  for services, **(10-10), 267**
 subcontractor information, **(10-05),**
  261-262; (10-06), 263
 telephone logs, **(10-07), 264;**
  (10-08), 265
 time
  analysis form, **(10-27), 289;**
   (10-28), 290

log, **(10-26), 288**
Referrals
 requesting, from client, **(4-43), 116**
 thanking client for **(4-44), 117**

S

Sales letters
 to clients, **(4-21), 79; (4-22), 80;**
  (4-23), 81; (4-24), 82;
  (4-25), 83
 following up after telemarketing,
  (4-07), 64; (4-08), 65;
  (4-09), 66
 to prospects, **(4-10), 67-68; (4-11),**
  69; (4-12), 70; (4-13), 71;
  (4-14), 72; (4-15), 73;
  (4-16), 74; (4-17), 75, (4-18),
  76; (4-19), 77; (4-20), 78
Selling services. *See* Marketing, direct
  methods; Marketing, indirect
  methods
Seminars. *See also* Public speaking
 giving, 121-123, **(5-03), 134-135;**
  (5-04), 136; (5-05), 137
Services, defining, 1-2
 statement of services, **(1-03), 7**
 worksheet for, **(1-02), 5-6**
Skills required for consulting, 1-3
 content, assessing **(1-01), 4**
 process, assessing **(1-04), 8-9**
Sole proprietorships
 advantages and disadvantages of,
  (2-01), 15-16
 described, 11
Speeches. *See* Public speaking; Seminars
Starting a business. *See also* Structure
  of businesses